ON YOUR OWN
(but not alone)

In and Around PHILADELPHIA

By Elizabeth Glaze

"Elizabeth Glaze encourages singles, couples and families to experience new activities and organizations with the help of her new resource book."
>Jenn Wilson
>**The Suburban and Wayne Times**

"A virtual encyclopedia of information. ...It's hard to imagine any area of human social activity that is not covered in this book."
>Len Lear
>**Chestnut Hill Local**

"When Elizabeth Glaze moved to the Philadelphia area in 1988 she approached building a life 'as though it were a second job.' ...Within three months, she felt at home. Now Glaze is passing out advice."
>Debra Nussbaum, Metropolis Column
>**Philadelphia Inquirer Sunday Magazine**

"A regional Baedecker brimming with helpful tips for both newcomers and longtime residents. ...It's about exploring new things and meeting people to do them with."
>Al Klimcke
>**Courier-Post**

ON YOUR OWN (but not alone) In and Around Philadelphia, 2nd Edition
Copyright ©1996 by Elizabeth Glaze
ISBN 0-9642482-2-0
Printed in the U.S.A.

Cover Design by FitzPatrick Design, Philadelphia

All rights reserved, including the right of reproduction in whole or in part in any form or by any electronic or mechanical means. No part of this book may be reproduced for distribution without written permission from the author or publisher, except by a reviewer, who may quote brief passages in a review.

For information or to order copies write:
Radnor-Hill Publishing, Inc.
P.O. Box 41051
Philadelphia, PA 19127

Or call
(215) 483-9556

The purpose of this book is to give readers a brief idea of what various agencies and groups in the area are like and have to offer. The author and publisher cannot be held responsible for any unintentional errors or omissions in this book. Inclusion in <u>ON YOUR OWN (but not alone)</u> does not imply unreserved endorsement of an organization or agency by the author, nor does exclusion imply disapproval. The author and publisher cannot be held responsible for any problems that may occur from a reader's subsequent involvement with any of the groups or agencies mentioned.

<u>**ON YOUR OWN (but not alone) accepts no advertising and is not beholden in any way to any commercial interest.**</u>

This book is dedicated to the friends and acquaintances who have helped me accumulate the information in it. In particular, I would like to thank my beloved Charles, my darling baby daughter "Nellie," my mother Dorothy, brother Peter and Debra Zahay who originally wanted to do this project together with me.

TABLE OF CONTENTS

	Page
Foreword From the Author	5
• TIPS "How to use this book"	6

SPECIAL INTEREST ORGANIZATIONS
Business / Professional Organizations	8
Computer Groups	13
Cultural / Artistic Interests	14
Handicrafts / Hobbies / Collectors	26
Life Interests Miscellaneous	30
Membership by Merit, Invitation or Audition	33
Nature / Animals / Conservation / Gardens	40
Philanthropic Groups	42
Political Interest Groups	43
Singles and Social Groups	44
Sports	54
Travel / Languages / Heritage Groups	76
Volunteer / Community Service Organizations	77

LOCAL SUPPORTIVE ORGANIZATIONS
Addiction Related	82
Disease or Injury Related	86
Divorced / Separated / In Mourning / Widowed	90
Family Group / Family Individuals / Children	94
Handicapped / Disabled Persons	101
Legal or Financial Advice	104
Men's and Women's Issues	107
New Residents	110
People Seeking Employment	113
Retired / Older Adults / Seniors	117

OTHER RESOURCES
Useful Hot Lines / Phone Numbers / Misc.	122
Useful Local Publications	123
Suggested Reading	131
• TIPS "How to write / answer a personal ad"	132
About Personal Ads and Dating Services	134

SPECIAL EVENTS / SEASONAL EVENTS
Summer Hangouts	138
Winter Hangouts	140
Some Fun Seasonal Events	142

INDEX
Index	149

ABOUT THE AUTHOR:

A resident of Pennsylvania since 1988, Elizabeth Glaze has lived in 5 countries, and in 5 states. Originally trained in both art and dance, she spent 9 years working and living in England, Austria, Germany and Switzerland as a professional ballet dancer.

Returning to the States and Manhattan in 1978, Elizabeth became a Personal Fitness Trainer. By 1985, her company "Personalized Fitness by Elizabeth Glaze" had grown to have 4 teaching assistants and 120 clients made up of doctors, models, socialites, average citizens and members of the British aristocracy.

Married in 1986, Elizabeth moved to Denver, Colorado and later to San Francisco, California. Unfortunately, the marriage was not a success.

Arriving in Philadelphia in late 1988, in the midst of divorce and with only 2 local acquaintances, Elizabeth began establishing a new life for herself. The first thing she did was look in the Yellow Pages under "Women." This led her to "The Women's Resource Center" and a subsequent divorce support group. Within 3 months, Elizabeth had a large circle of friends and acquaintances and a thriving social life. This was achieved through the weekly goal of attending at least one social activity (preferably a new one) each week, joining the mailing lists of many organizations, actively courting friendships with likable, supportive people and then introducing them to each other.

Currently, Elizabeth balances family life and a baby daughter with three careers. She manages to simultaneously work as a Personal Fitness Trainer, a Computer Graphics Artist/Trainer and as a writer.

From the moment she arrived in the area, Elizabeth began assembling information about groups, activities and organizations with the thought that others could benefit from her own happy experiences. This book is a result of that original plan.

FOREWORD

Do you feel like the last single person in your neighborhood?

Are you having trouble meeting other couples?

Has retirement left you feeling isolated?

Have you ever wondered how to find a support group?

Do you want to meet singles in settings other than at bars?

Have you ever wanted to join other novices in a new sport?

Then this book is meant for you!

Few people live their lives without ever feeling lonely. It may come as a result of moving, or divorce, or simply as a result of inner growth and a craving for new friends and experiences.

The fact is, a new social network is already out there waiting for you; you just have to know how to find it. This book will be your road map. If you set your mind to it, you can develop your social network quickly, with surprising ease, at any age, even on a limited budget.

When I moved here in 1988, I had 2 acquaintances in the area. Within 3 months I'd built a thriving social life and supportive circle for myself. However, I was also amazed at the number of people I met who were stuck in a social rut, bored or lonely when they were only minutes away from compatible groups and activities—all because they had no idea these groups or activities existed. That's why I decided to write this book.

I must warn you however, that my best efforts cannot guarantee that everything in this book will be accurate. Many organizations change their offerings and phone numbers frequently. And many of the groups listed have been visited by me or by friends, but it has not been possible to check all of them out in person. If you visit one of the groups mentioned and find the description inaccurate, please let me know.

I encourage readers to send information about groups and organizations that might be appropriate to add to the next edition! Write a detailed description and mail it to me, c/o Radnor-Hill Publishing, P.O. Box 41051, Philadelphia, PA, 19127. If I use quotes from your description, I will also mention your name and home town.

E. G.

TIPS: HOW TO USE THIS BOOK (with contributions from Debra Zahay)

1) Skim through the book to get an idea of the categories available. Keep an easy to read map of the Greater Philadelphia area beside you.

2) Select a primary goal. Do you want business connections, potential dates, pals to ski with or contact with other widowers? When I moved here, I just wanted lots of friends. Therefore, I spent my time trying dance groups, hiking groups, ski clubs, and doing things where I met *lots* of people on a steady basis. I felt that the *more* people I met per time invested, the more likely I was to find compatible friends.

3) Once you know your goal, look through the book and select relevant categories. Make notes in the margin of the book if you want to!

4) Call groups that interest you. Make sure they are still in existence and ask questions. Write down names of people you speak to in the margins of the book, and ask for names of other key people to look for at meetings (this provides you with instant acquaintances). After visiting a group, make notes in the margin before you forget any details.

5) Put your name on mailing lists, but don't join anything immediately. Most groups expect you to try them out a few times before becoming a member. Some groups never actually require you to join at all.

6) When you receive a flyer/newsletter from a group, write their activities and events down on your calendar. If you've just moved or are rebuilding your social life, it will make you feel good to see your calendar filled up with lots of potential events. I used to hang mine on the wall!

7) Set a 2nd goal. I disciplined myself to attend at least *one* activity per week and tried to attend something new each time. As I made friends, they would accompany me. Eventually I had a whole group to draw from, and they all came to know each other through me.

8) If a group/organization offers a variety of activities, try to attend at least 3 different ones. Different activities attract different members and show varying sides of the group. You may not be thrilled with members who turn up for a book lecture but you might love the ones who come out for a tennis party.

9) When you find a group you like, it's helpful to go to several events close together in time. Volunteering to do little things often helps you get to know people faster. One of my friends volunteered to man the punch bowl at the Christmas party of a group she hadn't even joined yet. Within an hour she'd met every single person at the party and one of the new acquaintances became her boyfriend.

Have fun!

SPECIAL INTEREST ORGANIZATIONS

In and Around
PHILADELPHIA

BUSINESS / PROFESSIONAL ORGANIZATIONS

HELPFUL HINTS: Membership in these organizations usually entitles you to their newsletters, their support network, the right to attend all of their activities, and group insurance if available. But lectures, seminars and dinner/buffet meetings often have an attendance fee (members pay less) with an average cost of $10–$35. Non-members are welcomed at most events so you can usually check groups out before you join. By the way, don't be surprised if the phone is answered with a different name; the groups are usually run by people who have corporate day jobs.

AMERICAN ASSOCIATION OF   (312) 280-0170
INDIVIDUAL INVESTORS, MAIN OFFICE
625 North Michigan Ave.
Chicago, IL 60611-3110
or,
Philadelphia Chapter Information Service   (610) 631-0208 (Hotline)

"A large, popular organization with meetings, seminars, and Special Interest Groups. The Philadelphia Chapter meets in the Valley Forge/ Main Line (Wayne) area. There are no chapters in Delaware or South Jersey. Memb. $49/yr.; additional costs can range from a $4 door fee to $30 for a pre-registered dinner with Peter Lynch lecturing. Call the local 'Information Service' hotline to learn of any meetings that are open to drop-in visitors. Or join directly through the main Chicago office (which handles all memberships and mailings), to immediately begin receiving newsletter and seminar registration information."

                            Charles Searle (a member)
                            Lafayette Hill, PA

ART DIRECTORS CLUB   (215) 569-3650
Philadelphia, PA

Covers topics relevant to advertising agencies, writers, photographers, graphic designers, educators, illustrators, art directors and free-lancers.

CHAMBER OF COMMERCE ORGANIZATIONS

Chamber of Commerce organizations exist to support local small businesses in almost every community. Membership offers group insurance rates and a supportive network. Activities include seminars, publications, volunteer groups and "card-exchange meetings" at which members and visitors swap business cards. Membership prices vary. The Greater Philadelphia Chamber of Commerce (215) 545-1234 offers a great variety of events and costs about $500/ yr., whereas The Main Line Chamber of Commerce (610) 687-6232 does things on a smaller scale and costs approx. $180/yr. Check your yellow or white pages for local groups. Non-members can attend events.

DIVERSIFIED INVESTOR GROUP   (215) 322-1175

An organization for people involved with or interested in real estate. Meets monthly on the last Thursday.

ENTREPRENEUR'S CLUB OF THE   (610) 630-0412
DELAWARE VALLEY
326 Rogers Road
Norristown, PA 19403

Support network for people with home-based businesses. Meetings are in the Jenkintown area once a month. Members network, hear lectures and take turns doing short presentations. New but growing quickly. Members receive newsletters. Memb./$20 every 6 months.

THE JAYCEES

"The Junior Chamber International (a Chamber of Commerce for young people). Members are 20–39 yrs., live or work near the branch they belong to, and many are single. They are a group that combines business networking with philanthropic activities. Events are attended by all ages. This is an organization in which a fairly upscale group of young people tirelessly raises money for everything from holiday fireworks displays to the Special Olympics and has a very good time doing it. The parties are good. Memb. approx. $45/yr. Has a newsletter. Admission to events is usually $15 or more. Official meeting and dinners are held monthly. **There are 26 Jaycee groups in the Delaware Valley.** Philadelphia is the only one with a permanent phone number (215) 972-3962. To contact the others, call your local Chamber of Commerce and ask how to reach the local Jaycees."

                        Mary Maki (event attendee)
                        Philadelphia, PA

JEWISH BUSINESS NETWORK   (215) 574-9280

Has a monthly luncheon meeting/lecture, usually on the 1st Wednesday of the month. $10 admission fee (includes lunch). Memb. is free.

LEADS CLUB
South New Jersey

An organization that provides networking opportunities for business professionals. They have the following meetings (all at 7 am): Tues. at the Ramblewood Country Club in Mt. Laurel, Thurs. at Ponzio's Diner in Cherry Hill (business women only), Tues. and Thurs. at the Sage Diner in Mount Laurel, and Thurs. at the IHOP in Berlin, NJ.

Le TIP
Warrington, PA

Local chap. of a nat'l network for business leads. They ask wholehearted commitment from members. Memb. is approx. $250/yr. They meet at the Warrington Motor Lodge every Wed. at 7:30 pm for a dinner and lecture.

NETWORKING PROFESSIONALS   (610) 902-1120
P.O. Box 384
Hatboro, PA 19040

Meets twice a month on Wednesday for breakfast in Horsham.
A relatively new group that shares leads and referrals. For businesses or professionals trying to expand their contacts. Nominal memb. fee/yr. Members pay for their own breakfast.

PENN. INNOVATION NETWORK (P.I.N.) (610) 647-6633
Malvern, PA

Pennsylvania Innovation Network. "For entrepreneurs and intrapreneurs exploring new technologies." Offers monthly meetings, seminars and help in applying for funding. Membership cost varies with size of company.

PEOPLE NETWORK (215) 946-8524
57 Neptune Lane
Levittown, PA 19054

Members of both sexes gather to socialize and network over breakfast on Sundays **in Yardley, PA**. Female members also meet for dinner once a month. Memb. $25/yr. (does not include cost of meals, but after you join, your first breakfast is free). You can attend once as a non-member.

PHILADELPHIA ADVERTISING CLUB (610) 874-8990
P.O. Box 12838
Philadelphia, PA 19108

Members are ad agency people, media people, representatives, production people and freelance artists. Memb. approx. $65/yr. They offer monthly meetings, holiday parties, summer outings, etc.

PHILADELPHIA ASSOCIATION
OF PART-TIME PROFESSIONALS
National Headquarters (Falls Church, VA) (703) 734-7975

The address for the Philadelphia group is: 2017 Laurel Rd., Havertown, PA 19083. Call the National Headquarters for literature. A networking group for people who work part-time or would like to. Meetings are held 4 times a year and are open to the public. Yearly membership $20/yr.

PHILADELPHIA WRITERS ORGANIZATION (215) 387-2244 (recording)
Philadelphia, PA (215) 387-4950 (messages)
Ardmore, PA (610) 649-8918

A business and networking group for writers. They have monthly meetings to discuss professionally-related topics and they also maintain a job bank. Attendance fee for non-members is approx. $10.

PROSPECTORS' CLUB OF CHERRY HILL (609) 667-0505

A business networking organization that meets every Wednesday at 7 am at Ponzio's Diner in Cherry Hill.

SMALL BUSINESS ASSOC. OF DEL. VALLEY (610) 237-1336

Holds bimonthly member breakfast meetings and seminars. They offer a resource directory, a newsletter, group insurance, and special information services for members who have a new business. Memb. $80/yr.

SOUTH JERSEY ENTREPRENEURS NETWORK (609) 429-0818
13 Tanner Street
Haddonfield, NJ 08033

Monthly programs, brown-bag lunch lectures and helpful services. 125 Members. Membership is $90 individual or $300 corporate memb./yr.

TEAMWORKS   (215) 545-7259
P.O. Box 15854
Philadelphia, PA 19103

Run by Phyllis Mufson. The organization is based on the premise that people achieve more professionally and personally when they are part of a motivating support team that meets regularly. Phyllis forms the teams and gets them started. She also runs "Idea Parties" in which attendees brainstorm for ideas and suggestions for each other.

SUNRISE NETWORK   (215) 368-1784
Plymouth Meeting, PA

Breakfast/networking/discussions for small-business owners. At the Inn at Plymouth Meeting, Fridays, 7 am. Reservations required.

TOASTMASTERS INTERNATIONAL   (714) 858-8255
World Headquarters
23182 Arroyo Vista
Rancho Margarita, CA 92688

An international organization that exists to help its members overcome shyness in social and public situations, improve their public speaking and communications skills and learn to network with each other. **There are groups all over the area; call to find the ones nearest you.** Some Toastmasters groups have dinner meetings and some simply have meetings. Membership price is usually $35/yr. or less. Members take turns giving assigned speeches (for which they receive supportive criticism), and work their way up through various levels of achievement.
Not surprisingly, there are many public figures and celebrities who are toastmasters, as well as business and non-business people.

BUSINESS GROUPS FOR WOMEN

AMERICAN BUSINESS WOMEN'S ASSOC.
A.B.W.A. National Office   (816) 361-6621
9100 Ward Parkway, P.O. Box 8728
Kansas City, MO 64114-0728

A.B.W.A. offers group insurance rates, scholarship/grant/loan opportunities and monthly meetings for dinner and networking. Membership is $27 (National level) plus $12 (local level)/yr. **Each chapter has a slightly different name and there are many in the area. Call or write the national office for current contact information.**

BUSINESS AND PROFESSIONAL WOMEN'S CLUB
B.P.W. National Office   (202) 293-1100
2012 Massachusetts Avenue,
N.W. Washington, DC 20036

They have branches in Philly, the Main Line, Upper Merion, Welsh Valley and Norristown among others. Local contact phone numbers change along with the club officers. Call or write the national office for current contact information. Members join the national and local organizations (approx. $60/yr.) and receive group insurance rate, scholarship, grant, loan and credit card opportunities.

GATHERINGS OF BUSINESS WOMEN   (215) 844-3018
4101 Kelly Drive
Philadelphia, PA 19129

For Delaware Valley Businesswomen, directed by Diane Carlson. **There are several groups around the area**; each meets at least once a month for breakfast. Twice a year all of the groups merge for a "TOGATHERNET" meeting, and once a year they all merge for a holiday celebration. Meetings usually feature a particular topic and speaker. The group offers contacts, start-up business resource information, group endeavors and group support. Memb. $65/yr. There is a newsletter and there are educational workshops. In late July they sponsor a "Women-Owned Business Fair." Meetings are open to non-members.

MONTGOMERY WOMEN'S NETWORK
Jeffersonville, PA

Meets once a month for networking and support. Keep an eye on local newspapers for meeting dates and contact numbers.

NAT'L ASSOC. OF FEMALE EXECUTIVES   (610) 526-0491 (Hotline)
Wayne, PA

A "Women's Interest Network." Part of a national organization. They have dinner meetings, in Wayne, the 3rd Wed. monthly. The group offers lectures with socializing and more. Call for details.

NATIONAL ASSOCIATION OF WOMEN   (215) 946-2773
BUSINESS OWNERS ("NAWBO")
513 Valmore Road
Fairless Hills, PA 19030

The National Association of Women Business Owners. They offer a newsletter, group insurance, networking/lecture meetings, breakfasts, luncheons, conventions and training seminars. When you join, you pay a national and a local chapter membership fee of $160/yr. Their meetings are usually in Center City.

PHILADELPHIA WOMEN'S NETWORK   (215) 946-1244
513 Valmore Road
Fairless Hills, PA 19030

For business and professional women. **Monthly meetings are in Center City** and involve socializing, dinner, a guest speaker and networking. They have a newsletter and other offerings. Memb. $45/yr.

WOMEN'S REFERRAL NETWORK   (610) 436-9222
OF CHESTER COUNTY
Exton Corporate Park
Exton, PA

Holds luncheons each month, either with a guest speaker or for the exchange of card and business literature. Memb. $70/yr. Non-members are welcome to attend. Susan Arnette is the contact person.

COMPUTER GROUPS

HELPFUL HINTS: The purpose of "User Groups" is to allow people to swap knowledge and tips. "PC" (Personal Computer) indicates that the group uses IBM (or clone) computers. "Mac" means Macintosh computers from Apple. I mention groups that have the most general appeal. There are MANY more in the Delaware Valley Computer User (for information see the Useful Publications category under *Other Resources*.)

ASSOCIATION OF PC PROFESSIONALS   (610) 668-9062
"For education of and networking among PC professionals." Monthly meeting locations vary from Ardmore to Center City to South Jersey.

BUXMONT COMPUTER USER GROUP   (215) 368-1949
Lansdale, PA
Meets the 2nd Thursday, monthly, in Lansdale. Supports IBM/Compaq.

BUX-MONT MAC USER GROUP   (215) 723-6900
109 Cobbler Court
Telford, PA 18969
Meets 1st Thursday, monthly, in Telford, PA. Memb. $15/yr.

DEL-CHES USER GROUP "Delchug"
P.O. Box 299
Lionville, PA 19353
Multi-support group that meets the last Saturday morning, monthly, in Wayne. Contact Modem Bulletin Board #(610) 363-6625 or write.

LOWER BUCKS COMPUTER USER GROUP   (215) 752-2705
Bristol, PA
"LUG" supports IBM, Mac, Amiga and Commodore. Meets the 1st Sunday afternoon, monthly, in Bristol, PA. Bulletin Board #(215) 946-1260.

MACINTOSH BUSINESS USERS SOCIETY   (215) 464-6600
P.O. Box 403
Huntingdon Valley, PA 19006-0403
Meets the last Wed., monthly, in Center City, Philly. Memb. is $35/yr.

MacUSER GROUP OF DELAWARE "MUD"   (302) 762-1814
P.O. Box 26231
Wilmington, DE 19899-6231
Meets the 3rd Tuesday, monthly, in Stanton, DE. Memb. $30/yr.

MacUSER GROUP OF S. NEW JERSEY   (609) 468-5000 x 20
Sewell, NJ   (609) 464-1551
Meets the last Wed., monthly, at Gloucester County College in Sewell.

MAIN LINE MACINTOSH USER GROUP   (610) 449-1227 (evenings)
570 Barton Lane
Wayne, PA 19087
Meets the 2nd Saturday at 9 am, monthly, in Paoli. Dues are $25–$35/yr.

PCP USERS GROUP (610) 519-7369
Wilmington, DE

PC group meets monthly at Concord Pike Library (north of Wilmington).

PC USER GROUP OF SOUTH JERSEY (609) 678-7179 (Hotline)
Cherry Hill, NJ

Has groups for Windows, OS/2, Graphics, Business, etc. Meets the 2nd Monday of each month, in Cherry Hill, NJ.

PHILADELPHIA AREA COMPUTER SOCIETY (215) 951-1255
Philadelphia, PA (University City)

"PACS" is approx. 60 separate user groups which meet the 3rd Saturday, monthly, at University City High School in Philly. Meeting times are staggered so it is possible to attend more than one. Memb. is $27/yr. (for the newsletter and other extras). Meetings are free. Call to ask for a schedule.

SOUTH JERSEY APPLE/MAC USER GROUP (609) 354-2135
P.O. Box 4273
Cherry Hill, NJ 08034-0649

"SJAUG" meets the 3rd Friday, monthly, in Medford. Mac and Apple II.

VALLEY FORGE COMPUTER CLUB "VFCC" (215) 878-9608
King of Prussia, PA

MSDOS users meet the 3rd Wednesday, monthly, in King of Prussia, PA.

CULTURAL / ARTISTIC INTERESTS

ARCHITECTURE

FOUNDATION FOR ARCHITECTURE (215) 569-3187
Philadelphia, PA (Center City)

A part of the American Institute of Architects. Offers visits to buildings, walking tours, meetings, conferences, exhibits and the Beaux Arts Ball. Maintains a bookshop and also asks for feedback from members regarding future building projects in the area. Memb. $25–$60/yr.

PHILADELPHIA SOCIETY FOR THE (215) 925-2251
PRESERVATION OF LANDMARKS
Philadelphia, PA (Center City)

Raises funds to maintain 4 historic buildings around Philadelphia by having parties and special events at them. The locations are beautiful; the parties very upscale (some are formal, some casual). Most events are $30 and up. Members pay less.

YOUNG MEMBERS OF THE PHILADELPHIA (same as above)
SOC. FOR THE PRESERVATION OF LANDMARKS

The members are under 35, upscale with a great deal of class. but are also genuinely nice. They give terrific parties, picnics, Easter egg hunts, etc. Most events cost $30; members pay less to attend.

FINE ART / FOLK ART

PHILADELPHIA ART ALLIANCE   (215) 545-4302
Philadelphia, PA (Center City)

Founded in 1915, they have a building on Rittenhouse Square and offer exhibits, lectures, performances, social events, parties, and a dining room for members and their guests. Membership comes in several categories. All events are free to members and most are open to the public at a small charge.

THE PHILADELPHIA FOLKLORE PROJECT   (215) 238-0096
Philadelphia, PA (Center City)

Offers exhibits, workshops and a newsletter involving folkart and folklife. Memb. approx. $10–$25/yr.

SAMUEL S. FLEISHER ART MEMORIAL   (215) 922-3456
709-721 Catharine St.
Philadelphia, PA 19147

Maintains an art gallery and offers free art classes and programs to adults and children. (However, they do ask them to try to make a contribution of $10–$25 each semester, depending on level of income.) The curriculum is substantial and the building is wonderful.

DANCING: ALL TYPES

PHILADELPHIA DANCE & MUSIC NETWORK   (610) 828-8918 (Hotline)
P.O. Box 1251
Bluebell, PA 19422

You can send $1 with a stamped, self-addressed envelope, and receive printed information. Or call the hotline and hear options on tape.
For example, you can ask to hear what dances are being held in the area. You can choose whether you want to hear about Folk, Contra, Square, Swing or Ballroom, etc. Another option is to find out where performances are being given (includes ballet). Music is another of several categories you can ask about. *Aside from the very first number you are asked to enter, which does not need a # sign, you must press the # sign after every choice or you won't get very far!*

DANCING: BALLROOM / SOCIAL DANCE

HELPFUL HINTS: Of course, there are numerous community night schools that offer social dancing instruction. Many ballroom dance schools also offer social dance nights that are open to the public for a small door fee. (Check the Bulletin Board listings in the "Neighbors" section of the Sunday <u>Philadelphia Inquirer</u>.)

GENERAL WAYNE INN   (610) 664-5125
Merion, PA

Offers ballroom dancing to live music. Fridays at 7:30 pm and Saturdays at 8 pm. Free admission.

GERSHMAN YM&YWHA　　　　　　　(215) 545-4400
Philadelphia, PA   (Center City)

Weekly on Wednesdays. A variety of dances from the rumba to the fox-trot are taught in hour-long sessions. Includes beginner, intermediate and advanced levels.

DANCING: COUNTRY WESTERN

80% of Country Western dances are line dances where individuals stand in rows. They step side to side, step back and forth, make a 1/4 turn and then repeat the whole series of steps again facing the new direction. The great freedom is that you can go to a club, surround yourself with people and frivolity, dance the entire night away and never talk to a single person unless you darn well want to. If you go often, you'll become familiar with other dance floor regulars and they'll become buddies to hang-out with (and help you remember dance steps). 20% of the dances consist of couples dances (often based on the two-step) but they are usually done intermittently.

Most clubs that offer Country Western dance also offer periodic lessons throughout the evening (they slowly talk everybody through a particular dance step and then gradually add music). Some clubs have specific days when they emphasize instruction. More and more clubs are cropping up all the time. I recommend that you ask around for one near you and call to ask about specifics before you go.

K. P. CORRAL　　　　　　　(610) 265-7234
King of Prussia Mall
King of Prussia, PA

This is a Country Western nightclub/bar that emphasizes instruction on Sunday afternoons. They do also have occasional instruction during the course of their regular evenings.

DANCING: FOLK / COUNTRY / CONTRA DANCE

HELPFUL HINTS: Attracts some of the nicest, most sincere people you will ever meet; often involved with teaching or computers. Rather than a shortage, there is usually an abundance of male partners for single females. Novices are very well treated and the first half hour or more is usually devoted to teaching newcomers the basics.

Contra Dancing and many Country Dance forms consist of repeated patterns and turns that are practiced without music until everyone is ready to do them. You'll meet a lot of people quickly because the choreography takes you to a new partner every two minutes.

An International Folk Dance, or Israeli Dance session usually starts off with leisurely paced line dances (everyone holds hands in a big circle). You learn a basic step and repeat it as you move to the right (or left), which makes the circle rotate. As the night wears on, the dance steps become more complicated. Couples dances are alternated with others, in which everyone dances in a fast moving circle (too fast to hold hands). By the end of the night the dances are so difficult that only the most experienced dancers know them, but by that time anyone who came early has already taken their tired little body home.

All of these forms of dance are excellent exercise; (dress in layers because you'll soon be peeling them off). Most places require soft-soled shoes (and high-heeled shoes are often forbidden because they damage floors!) Go to one dance evening and you'll learn about many of the others. Folk dancers often attend several weekly events.

FOLK DANCE COUNCIL OF THE DEL. VAL.   (215) 248-3521
7011 Sprague Street
Philadelphia, PA 19119

Gives out a flyer listing the days and locations of many member folk dance organizations in the area. (Most of them meet weekly.) Promotes international folk dance and music. Memb. $8–$13/ yr. Most of the groups I have listed are members of the council.

MONDAY

AMERICAN, ENGLISH AND SCOTTISH   (609) 779-9084
COUNTRY DANCING
Pineland Country Dancers
Westfield Friends School
Cinnaminson, NJ

Dancing and instruction weekly, from September to June. Door fee.

TUESDAY

INTERNATIONAL FOLK DANCING   (215) 945-1316
Art Museum Terrace
Philadelphia, PA (Center City)

Weekly from spring through late September. Sneakers recommended. Beginners welcome. Small admission fee.

ISRAELI FOLK DANCING   (215) 698-7300
"Cafe Israel"   (215) 671-9761
Klein Branch, YWHA
Philadelphia, PA (Northeast)

These weekly dances are targeted towards beginners. Small fee.

WEDNESDAY

ENGLISH COUNTRY DANCING   (215) 247-5993
Germantown Country Dancers
Calvary Episcopal Church
Philadelphia, PA (Germantown)

Starts with lessons for novices, and progresses into elaborate dances. Meets 2nd, 4th and 5th Wednesdays, monthly (except in Aug.). Small fee.

INTERNATIONAL FOLK DANCING   (215) 572-2153
Beaver College   (215) 233-9399 before 8:30 pm
Glenside, PA

Weekly dances start off with lessons for novices, and progress into more elaborate dances. Small admission fee.

INTERNATIONAL FOLK &   (302) 764-2682
WESTERN SQUARES DANCING
Arden Guild Hall
Arden, DE

Weekly dances start off with lessons for novices and progress into more elaborate dances. Small admission fee.

ISRAELI FOLK DANCING   (215) 545-4400
Gershman YMHA.
Philadelphia, PA (Center City)

Weekly dances. Small admission fee.

THURSDAY

CONTRA DANCING   (215) 844-3259
Summit Presbyterian Church
Philadelphia, PA (Mt. Airy)

Weekly dances start off with lessons for novices, and progress into more elaborate dances. Small admission fee.

ISRAELI FOLK DANCING   (609) 665-6100
Cherry Hill Jewish Community Center
Cherry Hill, NJ

Dances held weekly. Small admission fee.

ISRAELI FOLK DANCING   (215) 671-9761
"Cafe Israel"
Philadelphia Art Museum
Philadelphia, PA

Warmer months only; weekly, on the Art Museum terrace. Starts with lessons for novices and progresses into more difficult dances. Small fee.

FRIDAY

CONTRA DANCING   (609) 882-7733
Lambertville Country Dancers "LCD"
Yardley Community Center
Lambertville, PA

Meets the 2nd and 4th Fridays of each month. Small admission fee.

ENGLISH COUNTRY DANCING   (609) 882-7733
Lambertville Country Dancers "LCD"
Titusville Methodist Church
Titusville, NJ

Meets the 1st Friday of each month. Small admission fee.

INTERNATIONAL FOLK DANCING   (215) 624-4242
St. Michael's Lutheran Church
Philadelphia, PA (Germantown)

Weekly dances start with lessons for novices. Small admission fee.

INTERNATIONAL FOLK DANCING   (609) 893-6138
Westfield Friends School
Cinnaminson, NJ

Meets 2nd, 4th and 5th Fridays, monthly. Starts with a lesson. Small fee.

IRISH DANCING / Philadelphia Ceili Group   (215) 849-8899 (Hotline)
Commodore Barry Club   (215) 843-8051
Philadelphia, PA (Mount Airy)

Irish dancing every week. Small admission fee.

SCOTTISH COUNTRY DANCING   (215) 248-5998
Grace Episcopal Church
Philadelphia, PA (Mt. Airy)

Two dances a month. Novices and experts. Small fee (first session free).

SCOTTISH COUNTRY DANCING   (610) 565-2110
held at a private home
Moylan, PA (near Media)

Novices and experts dance twice a month. Small fee (first session free).

SATURDAY

CONTRA DANCING   (215) 860-8175
Summit Presbyterian Church
Philadelphia, PA (Mt. Airy)

Starts with a lesson. Meets 3rd Saturday monthly. Small admission fee.

INTERNATIONAL FOLK DANCING   (215) 945-1316
Westfield Friends School
Cinnaminson, NJ

Starts with a lesson. Meets 1st and 3rd Saturdays monthly. Small fee.

SUNDAY

CAJUN DANCING   (215) 576-0839
Arden Guild Hall
Arden, DE

Starts with a lesson. 3rd Sunday afternoon, monthly. Small fee.

CONTRA DANCING   (302) 654-1368
Arden Guild Hall
Arden, DE

1st Sunday afternoon, monthly. Starts with lesson. Small admission fee.

ISRAELI FOLK DANCING   (215) 698-7300
Klein Branch, YMHA   (215) 671-9761
Philadelphia, PA (Northeast)

Weekly evening dances start with instruction for novices. Small fee.

DANCING: SQUARE DANCE

HELPFUL HINTS: If a club or church has a square dance, you'll meet everyone there, since you are constantly being asked to, "move to the next partner" while dancing. Usually, the male/female ratio is fairly equal. Organizations that are BASED entirely around square dancing are much more serious about it and ask beginners to take periodic lessons they offer before joining large group dances. It is not unusual to find families of 3 generations involved with square dancing. Often, the men wear western style clothing, while the women wear huge petticoats under a full skirt. In any case, you'll get a great workout and meet nice people.

DANCE! Magazine
Ed Armon
317 Dalton Street
Philadelphia, PA 19111-1802

This magazine lists all the square dance clubs and special events in the Delaware Valley and surrounding area. $11.50/yr. (10 issues per year).

THE DELAWARE VALLEY FEDERATION 1(800) 892-8828
OF SQUARE AND ROUND DANCERS

The Federation has divided the Delaware Valley into several districts. The square dance clubs that fall within a geographic area report to the chairperson of that district. Call the Federation and tell them what area you live in; **they'll** either **tell you about the clubs in your area** or give you the name and number for the chairperson of your district.

CLUB SASHAY (610) 566-6552
Springfield, PA

Dances held 2nd and 4th Saturdays, monthly. For "Plus Level" square dancers, with round dancing as well. Wide age range of participants. Free refreshments. Memb. $35–70/yr. or pay door fee of $8 per couple.

KING SQUARE DANCE CLUB (610) 265-7847 or
Wayne, PA (610) 692-6067

For dancers at the "Plus Level." Instruction for beginners and lower level dancers starts in September. All ages participate.

TUESDAY NIGHT SQUARE DANCE GUILD (215) 477-8434
St. Mary Parish Hall, University of Pennsylvania
Philadelphia, PA   (University City)

Dances held 2nd Tuesday, monthly. Live music, free refreshments. No experience or partner necessary. Small fee.

DANCING: SWING DANCE

HELPFUL HINTS: Has a fairly good male/female ratio and attracts people from a wide variety of interests and backgrounds (conservative business types next to 1960's era looking types). Live bands play (sometimes with singers). If you get there at the very beginning there will be instruction on the (extremely easy) basic swing dance step. (The idea is to gradually learn fancier variations of it). The people who run the dances are usually extremely helpful and will often take the time to teach you a few of the fine points, if asked. The women often wear skirts that flare out when they turn. Wear soft soled shoes and no high heels!!!

PHILADELPHIA SWING DANCE SOCIETY   **(215) 576-0345 (Ans. Machine)**
Philadelphia, PA (Mount Airy)
Founded by 12 people who adore Swing Dance/Lindy/Jitterbug. The 2 times per month dances have live music and a nice, fun atmosphere. Holiday dance parties are jammed. No partner necessary. Admission is approx. $8 (less if you bring baked goods for the refreshments).

LITERATURE / POETRY

BOOKSTORE EVENTS
I believe the whole thing was started by Philadelphia's Borders Bookstore when they built an espresso bar and began offering poetry readings and performances. Then they opened other branches with the same offerings. Now, bookstores like Barnes & Noble, Gene's Books and Encore Books seem to be offering everything from book discussions to ballroom dancing lessons. For information check your local bookstores.

GREAT BOOKS DISCUSSION GROUPS
Call your local library to ask about groups in your area. Twice a month, a trained leader heads a discussion of pre-specified books. (Free)

NEW JERSEY POETRY SOCIETY   **(609) 751-1841**
Vorhees, NJ
Meets 1st Wed. monthly, 7 pm, in Vorhees. Poets read their poems for open critique, enter competitions. Memb. $3/yr. Contact person is Laura.

PHILADELPHIA WRITERS ORGANIZATION   **(215) 387-2244 (Recording)**
Philadelphia, PA   **(215) 387-4950 (Messages)**
Ardmore, PA   **(610) 649-8918**
Business and networking group for writers. Monthly meetings on professionally related topics. They maintain a job bank. Refreshments are usually served at meetings. Attendance fee for non-members is approx. $10.

THEATER CENTER PLAYWRIGHTS   **(215)336-3869 (Hotline)**
Philadelphia, PA
This group meets once a week in Center City to read and critique their scripts. They are the oldest writer's group in the Delaware Valley.

WRITER'S CLUB OF DELAWARE COUNTY   **(610) 259-0895**
367 Fairfax Rd.
Drexel Hill, PA 19026
Meets the 4th Tuesday monthly, in Springfield. Have 4 ongoing groups (poetry, articles and fiction) that meet monthly as well. Memb. $25/yr.

POETRY AND LITERARY FORUM   **(215) 685-0592**
Philadelphia, PA (Northeast)
Guest readers with an open forum afterwards. Every other Saturday.

MOVIES / CINEMA

HELPFUL HINTS These organizations attract people who love films. After awhile it becomes easy to spot the regulars and say "Hi."

CONNELLY CENTER (610) 645-4750
Villanova, PA

Runs a cultural/classic film series at Villanova University.

FILMBILL RENDEZVOUS
46 North Front Street
Philadelphia, PA 19106

Single movie lovers meet every other Sun. for a film viewing at the Ritz, and discussion afterwards. For more info. send $5, name and address.

FILM FORUM SOCIETY (215) 732-7704
Philadelphia, PA (Center City)

Classic films are shown regularly; members pay reduced admission rates. Call if you want to be on their mailing list.

INTERNATIONAL CINEMA (215) 387-5125
International House
Philadelphia, PA (University City)

A seasonal film series. Current social topics, independent filmmaker projects and world cinema. Call to be on the mailing list.

TALK CINEMA (Harlan Jacobson's) 1(800) 551-9221
116 Pinehurst Ave. C33
New York, NY 10033

"Sneak Preview" screening series (7 Saturdays) twice a year for members (many are single) in Philadelphia with discussion after. 120 members and growing. Films are commercial art films or independent productions.

MUSEUMS

BRANDYWINE RIVER MUSEUM (610) 388-7601
P.O. Box 141
Chadds Ford, PA 19317

Members receive invitations to openings of exhibits, trips, the annual children's Christmas party and more. Memb. $30–$40/yr.

YOUNG FRIENDS OF THE B.R.M. (same as above)
(same address as above)

Young members (age 18–40) have additional events: An annual party, environmental activities, concerts, family events, outings. Memb. $45/yr.

THE FRANKLIN INSTITUTE (215) 448-1231
Membership Office
Benjamin Franklin Parkway at 20th St.
Philadelphia, PA 19103-9934

Events, exhibit previews, etc. The "Galaxy Ball" is only open to members at a higher membership rate. Regular membership is ($35–$65/yr.).

FRIENDS OF THE PHILADELPHIA   (215) 684-7822
MUSEUM OF ART
P.O. Box 7646
Philadelphia, PA 19101-7646

Membership is $100, which automatically covers 2 people (meaning you can bring a spouse or friend to the various events offered).

YOUNG FRIENDS OF THE   (same as above)
PHILADELPHIA MUSEUM OF ART
(same address as above)

For people under age 35. This is a branch of the "Friends of Philadelphia Museum of Art" that has additional events, with activities that are singles oriented, innovative and very upscale. Memb. $50/yr.

MUSIC (PARTICIPATORY)

CLASSICAL

AMATEUR CHAMBER MUSIC PLAYERS   (212) 645-7424
545 8th Avenue, 9th floor
New York, NY 10018

Publishes a national directory of self-rated amateur chamber music groups, the purpose being that they can be contacted by musicians living or traveling in their area, for chamber music "Jam sessions."

FOLK

DELAWARE VALLEY FOLK MUSIC ALLIANCE   (215) 732-9992 (Hotline)
Philadelphia, PA (Center City)

Offers concerts, pot-luck dinner meetings and singing sessions.

PHILADELPHIA FOLKSONG SOCIETY   (215) 247-1300
Philadelphia, PA (Mount Airy)

Holds monthly "Sings" (everyone vocalizes with/without instruments), house concerts, workshops, and "Concert Meetings." Memb. $15–30/yr.

SONG WRITING

NJ/PA SONGWRITERS ASSOCIATION
Cherry Hill, NJ

For beginners and professionals. They meet the 4th Tuesday of each month at 7:00 pm in the Cherry Hill Free Library. Memb. $25/yr. individuals, $35/yr. for bands. Attendance at the 1st meeting is free.

SONG WRITER'S FORUM   (215) 685-0592
Philadelphia, PA (Northeast)

Sponsored by the Philadelphia Cultural Council. Meetings are the 3rd Mon. monthly (Sept.–June), at the Northeast Regional Library. Call to be on the mailing list. Meetings have guest song writers, and lyricists speak on appropriate topics. Some meetings are scheduled to be an open forum for the public to present their work.

SINGING

HELPFUL HINTS: The most obvious way to join a chorus is to find a church chorus and ask to join it. Local colleges often maintain a chorus which you can join. The following groups do not require an audition.

DELAWARE VALLEY CHORAL SOCIETY (215) 295-8080
Langhorne, PA

This chorus of 60 volunteers performs classical, religious and show tunes. Membership is open to all; only soloists must audition.

PENNSYLVANIA PRO MUSICA (215) 222-4517
Philadelphia, PA (Center City)

Holds a public "Sing In" once a year on New Year's Eve. An $8 fee pays for entry and a copy of the music. For those who want to spend an additional $50, the rehearsal and subsequent sing-in are followed by a champagne gala and buffet.

ROSEMONT COLLEGE COMMUNITY CHORUS (610) 527-0200, X236
Rosemont, PA

All residents of the community are invited to join the choir.

SINGING CITY (215) 561-3930
Philadelphia, PA

Holds public "Sing-Ins" of large choral pieces such as the "Messiah." Pay $8 for entry and you'll receive a book of words and music to sing from.

THEATRE / DANCE / MUSIC (NON-PARTICIPATORY)

HELPFUL HINTS: Remember, if you would love to be more than just a part of the audience, but can't sing, act, dance or play a note, community theater groups also need volunteers back-stage. Non-singing members build sets, make costumes, props, and work backstage during performances. If this sounds interesting to you, you might also want to check out the groups listed under the category titled "Membership by Merit, Invitation or Audition."

DELAWARE VALLEY OPERA COMPANY (215) 424-5980
Roxborough, PA

A repertory opera company based in a house in Fairmount Park. They hold: outdoor performances in the summer, indoor concert events in the winter, 3 theme dinners with Italian, French or "other" music, and a New Year's party. The backstage crew is made up of invaluable non-singing members, as is part of the audience. Memb. approx. $15/yr.

THE LIVELY ARTS GROUP (215) 567-3339
Architects Building, Suite 1400
117 South 17th Street
Philadelphia, PA 19103

Visits local events, makes bus trips to Broadway shows and operas at the Met, and tours historic locations. Quarterly newsletter. Memb. $15–$20/yr. (Non-members may also come along.)

OPERA APPRECIATION CLUB (610) 828-6641
Lafayette Hill, PA

Meets one Friday a month, over coffee and cake, to watch a pre-recorded opera and discuss it. They attend operas as a group on a regular basis. $1 attendance fee pays for the coffee and cake.

THE OPERA CLUB (215) 322-1364
Philadelphia, PA

Sponsors various events, lectures and performances to do with opera.

THE ORPHEUS CLUB (215) 546-6648
254 S. Van Pelt
Philadelphia, PA

Associate Members of the club are of both sexes and attend several events a year as listeners to the Orpheus Club's all male chorus. One performance is held at the club house and is done in period costume.

PENNSYLVANIA BALLET COMPANY (215) 551-7000
1101 South Broad Street
Philadelphia, PA 19147

As a member, it is possible to become involved behind the scenes. The ballet has two volunteer organizations for fund raising:
The "Corps De Voluntaires" organizes the annual Christmas party gala.
The "Volunteer Guild" hosts open rehearsals, open houses, receptions.

THE PHILADELPHIA OPERA GUILD (215) 928-2108
510 Walnut Street
Philadelphia, PA

Members support the opera company by organizing annual holiday fund-raiser parties, dinners, galas and receptions.

THE PHILADELPHIA OPERA JUNIOR GUILD (215) 928-2108

Members (age 35 and younger), receive a special subscription rate and invitations to annual parties, events, and post-opera dinners.

THE PHILADELPHIA ORCHESTRA ASSOC. (215) 893-1999
1420 Locust Street, Suite 320
Philadelphia, PA 19102-4297

The association has approx. 12 geographically based committees. They organize various fund-raisers throughout the year. Call for more info.

YOUNG FRIENDS OF THE (215) 893-1999
PHILADELPHIA ORCHESTRA

Age 35 and younger. They offer several events each year (picnics and parties) and often have arrangements of their own at fund-raisers (like the annual Academy Ball in January). Call for more information.

SETTLEMENT MUSIC SCHOOL (215) 885-3345
OPERA TRIPS and APPRECIATION CLASSES
515 Meetinghouse Rd.
Jenkintown, PA 19046

Organizes trips to concerts and operas in various cities. $10 puts you on their "1st Class" mailing list. Call for details.

HANDICRAFTS / HOBBIES / COLLECTORS

HANDICRAFTS

THE AMERICAN SEWING GUILD, Nat'l HQ   (503) 772-4059
P. O. Box 8476   (503) 770-7041 (Fax)
Medford, OR 97504-0476

"For anyone interested in sewing, crafts or related arts." Call to find local chapters; (then ask the chapter about neighborhood groups near you.)

THE EMBROIDERERS GUILD OF AMERICA   (502) 589-6956
335 North Broadway, Suite 100
Louisville, KY 90202

There are several chapters in the Delaware Valley. Contact the national organization for phone numbers of local groups in your area. Groups generally meet regularly to discuss their craft and help beginners.

PHILADELPHIA GUILD OF HAND WEAVERS   (215) 487-9690 (Hotline)
Philadelphia, PA (Manayunk)

I am told that this is the only weaving group in the U.S. with a permanent location/phone number. They offer monthly meetings and classes. They also support crafts related to weaving, such as dying and spinning. Members come from many surrounding areas, but if you need to find a group closer to you, they'll tell you how to contact "M.A.F.A." (the Mid-Atlantic Fiber Assoc.) to locate other groups.

SMOCKING ARTS GUILD OF AMERICA   (708) 390-SAGA
4350 DiPaolo Center, Suite C
Dearlove Road
Glenview IL, 60025

They "preserve and foster the art of smocking and related needlework for future generations." Contact the national organization for info. on local groups. The Main Line has one called the Greene Countrie Smockers. They meet once a month to hear a guest speaker, work on group projects, and give tips to beginners. They also have picnics and holiday parties.

QUILTING GUILDS

The National Quilting Assoc. is at P.O. Box 393, Ellicott City, MD 21041-0393. (301) 461-5733. They can tell you if any of their member groups is in your area. However, not all quilting groups are members and so you might also contact local quilt, sewing and crafts shops to locate groups. Groups generally meet monthly. Smaller groups of members form quilting bees that meet more often. In Sept., the Fort Washington Convention Center has a huge quilt show and all of the clubs go to it.

QUILTERS OF THE ROUND TABLE   (215) 748-7700
Philadelphia, PA (Center City)

An Afro-American quilting club that meets monthly. Non-Afro-Americans are also members. Some members use traditional styles and others experiment with African designs and fabrics. Contact Christina Johnson.

HOBBIES

AIRPLANE MODEL FLYING

VALLEY FORGE SIGNAL SEEKERS
857 Durant Court
West Chester, PA 19380-1723

Meets at a flying field in Valley Forge Park (just off Route 252 near the PA turnpike). Members must join the AMA (see below) and be certified.

ACADEMY OF MODEL AERONAUTICS   (703) 435-0750
1810 Samuel Morse Drive
Reston, VA 22090

Call them to find out about groups near you. They certify members.

ASTROLOGY

PHILADELPHIA ASTROLOGICAL SOCIETY   (215) 643-6597
Philadelphia, PA

Monthly meetings one Friday each month at International House. Also offers workshops and special events. Meetings often involve a lecture by someone of national interest. Memb. $30/yr. Ask for Linda Waters.

ASTRONOMY

DEL. VALLEY AMATEUR ASTRONOMERS   (215) 836-9266

Offers telescope viewing nights, often in Roxborough or Valley Forge Park.

BUCKS-MONT ASTRONOMICAL ASSOC.   (215) 579-9973

Periodic sky watch nights for the public in and around Doylestown.

BEER HOME BREWING

"Traditional beers, made by regional craft breweries have grown rapidly in popularity. To meet people with an interest in beer and brewing, as well as to participate in beer-related competitions, events and outings there are several clubs in the greater Philadelphia area. They are typically low cost or free and are sponsored by homebrew supplies stores. Contact them for more information on meetings and events."

                        Peter Stephinson (a home brewer)
                        Lafayette Hill, PA

BEER UNLIMITED   (610) 397-0666
515 Fayette Street
Conshohocken, PA 19428

BEER UNLIMITED   (610) 889-0905
Great Valley Shopping Center
Malvern, PA 19355

Both of the Beer Unlimited stores have clubs called B.U.Z.Z. (Beer Unlimited Zany Zymurgists.) They meet at least once a month.

Page 28

HOME SWEET HOMEBREW   (215) 569-9469
2008 Sansom Street
Philadelphia, PA 19103

This shop has a club called H.O.P.S. They meet at least once a month.

KEYSTONE HOMEBREW SUPPLY   (610) 855-0100
779 Bethlehem Pike
Montgomeryville, PA 18396

Their club is called Keystone Hops and they meet at least once a month.

CHESS

U. S. CHESS FEDERATION   (914) 562-8350
186 Route 9W
New Windsor, NY 12553

This national organization can send you a list of clubs in your area.

FAN CLUBS/ENTHUSIAST CLUBS

NATIONAL FANTASY FAN CLUB   (610) 353-3698
The Castle Keepers Chapter, P.O. Box 281
Broomall, PA 19008

Disneyana enthusiasts meet monthly, discuss potential collector items, and party. Very family oriented. They also attend movies. Memb. $15/yr.

SONS OF THE DESERT   (215) 657-0111
Huntingdon Valley, PA

For Laurel & Hardy fans. Banquets, films and entertainment 3 times a year. Part spoof, part serious, their funds support charity. Memb. $20/yr.

FISHING

HELPFUL HINTS: For other groups check with local equipment stores.

SURF ANGLERS ASSOCIATION   (215) 249-9779
Warminster, PA

Meets monthly at the Warminster Rec. Center. Members go on informal trips, participate in tournaments. Memb. $36/yr. plus $5 initiation.

TROUT UNLIMITED & FLY FISHERS   (215) 348-0876
Doylestown, PA

Meets monthly at the Doylestown Courthouse. Memb. $10/yr.

HAM RADIO

AMERICAN RADIO RELAY LEAGUE   (203) 666-1541
225 Main Street
Newington, CT 06111

An ex-boyfriend's ham radio obsession first introduced me to this group. There are local groups in Philadelphia and Villanova among others. Call to ask for contacts. The local clubs will help you train, certify and register.

JUGGLING

JUGGLERS CLUB (610) 383-8898
375 East Chestnut St.
Coatesville, PA 19320

All skill levels meet Mondays at 6 pm and it's free. They are at the Art Museum steps in summer and in Memorial Hall in Winter. Equipment and unicycles are available for practice at the sessions. They also socialize and attend juggling festivals. Contact person is Dick Rainer.

KITE FLYING

I don't know of any groups yet, but locations that kite flyers seem to gravitate to include Valley Forge Park (up the road from the Visitor's Center) and Cape May beach on the Jersey Shore. There is also an annual Kite Festival every April in Philadelphia. Call (215) 685-0052 for details.

MAGICIANS

SOCIETY OF AMERICAN MAGICIANS (215) 364-8132
4751 Weldon Avenue
Trevose, PA 19053

A national organization, 120 local members. Memb. $55/yr. Meets 3rd Thurs. monthly in NE Philly. Lectures, parties, workshops, competitions.

SOCIETY OF YOUNG MAGICIANS (215) 342-4647
1310 Fanshawe Street
Philadelphia, PA 19111

For kids 7–16 yrs. 2nd & 4th Thurs. monthly in Warminster. $15/yr.

PHOTOGRAPHY & VIDEO

HELPFUL HINTS: Local camera shops can often suggest local clubs.

THE PHOTOGRAPHIC SOCIETY OF PHILA. (215) 843-3868
Philadelphia, PA (609) 488-4657

The oldest camera club in the U.S. Meets monthly for lectures, outings, demonstrations, holiday parties and exhibits. Memb. $30/yr.

SUBURBAN PHILADELPHIA VIDEO CLUB (215) 379-0222
Jenkintown, PA

This amateur group helps members produce high quality home videos. Meets 4th Wed. monthly at Jenkintown Library. $25/yr. memb.

SCIENCE FICTION

PHILADELPHIA SCIENCE FICTION SOCIETY (215) 957-4004 (Hotline)
Philadelphia, PA

For fans of science fiction. Members attend movies, discuss books and have get-togethers. They meet at International House in Philly, the 2nd Friday of each month at 8:00 pm.

SCRABBLE

PHILADELPHIA AREA SCRABBLE CLUB (610) 586-8488
  (215) 676-5636
Meets to play at 4 different locations. Games follow NSA rules.

SJ SCRABBLE CLUB (609) 728-9446
Berlin, NJ
All skill levels. Meets on Thurs. and Sat. at the Berlin Baptist Church.

COLLECTORS

STAMPS

THE COLLECTORS CLUB OF PHILADELPHIA (610) 828-8631
Box 176
Lafayette Hill, PA 19444
Meets the first Tuesday, monthly, in Lafayette Hill for lectures/demos.

LIFE INTEREST MISCELLANEOUS

FOOD

AMERICAN INSTITUTE OF WINE & FOOD (215) 635-4463 (Hotline)
P.O. Box 643
Jenkintown, PA 19046

A local chapter of a national organization founded by Julia Child and Robert Mondavi. They alternate food and beverage (wine, beer, coffee) events. The avg. cost is $35. The 246 members are 50/50: pros and food fans, couples and singles, males and females. Memb. $60/yr.–$125/yr.

THE COUPLE GOURMET (215) 732-0260
1003 Walnut Street, Box 520 (215) 732-2008 Fax
Philadelphia, PA 19103

Gourmet social events for couples at local restaurants. There are various monthly events and occasional trips to other towns.

INTERNATIONAL WINE CLUB "IWC" (610) 649-9936 (Hotline)
P.O. Box 1478
Havertown, PA 19083

Meets 2–4 times a month in Philly for "Walk-around" and seminar wine tastings. Full memb. $200/yr. ($300 for couples), Select memb. $50/yr.

VEGETARIAN SOCIETY OF SOUTH JERSEY (609) 354-0909
P. O. Box 272
Marlton, NJ 08053

They have monthly meetings, group projects, cooking classes, picnics, pot-lucks. They have special interest sub-groups (one is for singles). Memb. $12–$25/yr.

VEGETARIANS OF PHILADELPHIA (215) 276-3198
P. O. Box 24353
Philadelphia, PA 19120

Monthly meetings for lectures, picnics, workshops, outings. They have a newsletter and a singles sub-group. 270 Members. Memb. $16/yr.

HEALTH

The CPR classes are brimming with female nurses. You practice on dummies but work with partners. If you're a male, the odds are in your favor.

THE AMERICAN HEART ASSOCIATION (610) 940-9540
Conshohocken, PA

THE AMERICAN RED CROSS (215) 299-4000
Philadelphia, PA

HOMEOPATHY STUDY

NATIONAL CENTER FOR HOMEOPATHY (703) 548-7790
801 North Fairfax Street, Suite 306 (703) 548-7792
Alexandria, VA 22314

Learn the ancient practice of treating illness with natural medicines. Call for a group near you; I know of one in Conshohocken. Memb. $35/yr.

KIDS

HELPFUL HINTS: Also, there are at least 3 local books and 3 magazines for parents of children in the Delaware Valley (listed under Useful Local Publications in the *Other Resources* category).

DEPARTMENTS OF RECREATION/DEPARTMENTS OF PARKS

Most townships and counties have one department or the other, or a combination of the two. They always offer/coordinate a vast number of activities for children and adults and often run Community Centers too. They can tell you about activities they organize and run, and help you contact groups that use their facilities or grounds. For example, the Little League usually makes arrangements with them and so they can often tell you how to get in touch with your local Little League group.

My neighborhood Recreation Department sends out flyers every season. In February they offer: Basketball and Softball leagues for boys and girls, Learn-to-swim lessons, Computer tots programs, "Kid's Corner" (ages 4–6), Gymnastics, Karate and Recreational swimming. In summer they offer: a Playground program, a Pre-school program (age 4–6), Track-n-field, Tennis lessons, Amusement park discount tickets, Computer tots programs, Field hockey, Soccer, Concerts in the park, Morning lap swims, and an Open gym for high schoolers.

BOY SCOUTS Philadelphia (215) 988-9811

Memb. is $7/ yr. Call for information on your local chapter:
Cub Scouts are 7–10, Boy Scouts 11–13. Explorers are high school age.

GIRL SCOUTS Philadelphia (215) 564-4657
Memb. is $6/yr. Call for information on your local chapter: Daisy Girl Scouts are age 5, Brownies Girl Scouts 6–8, Junior Girl Scouts 9–11, Cadette Girl Scouts 12–14 and Senior Girl Scouts are 15–17.

POLICE ATHLETIC LEAGUE ("PAL") (215) 426-5206
Main Headquarters
Belgrade & Clearfield Streets.
Philadelphia, PA   19134

The PAL youth program involves boys and girls, age 8–18, and offers a wide range of sports, cultural and recreational activities. Call the main headquarters to ask how to contact your local branch.

THE YM & YWCA
Originally "Young Christian Associations" for men and women, these organizations are now co-ed, with members from every religion and age group. They offer everything from swimming lessons for babies to activity oriented support groups. You will find them in the phone book.

THE YM & YWHA
Originally "Young Hebrew Associations" for men and women, they now offer completely non-sectarian activities for people of all ages along with activities for Jewish members. They are just as likely to attract a mixed crowd for volleyball as they are to offer Israeli folk dancing. They have lots of activities for children and their parents. Now a part of a much bigger organization, the YM & YWHAs in this area are also Jewish Community Centers (JCCs). You will find them listed under Jewish Community Centers in the phone book.

JEWISH COMMUNITY CENTERS (JCCs)
See the description for YM & YWHA.

RELIGION

Those of you who adhere to better known religions can open up your local yellow pages to "Churches" or "Synagogues" and locate your nearest congregation. These are two alternative organizations.

ETHICAL CULTURE SOCIETY (215) PE5-3456
1906 S. Rittenhouse Sq.
Philadelphia, PA   19103

Members, who come from many backgrounds and religions, do not have to give up personal beliefs in order to join. The society holds services and social events (as in a church or synagogue); their main goal is to promote ethics, moral standards and toleration of individual opinions.

PHILADELPHIA BUDDHIST ASSOCIATION (610) 660-9269
6 Old Lancaster Rd (near City Line Avenue)
Merion, PA

Provides nonsectarian meditation, instruction, discussion and guest speakers. Meetings are 2 nights a week. Membership is not required.

MEMBERSHIP BY: MERIT, INVITATION OR AUDITION

HELPFUL HINTS: Yes, these organizations require that you be invited to join by one or more of their current members but it's not necessarily for snobbish reasons. All clubs and groups pride themselves on having a certain individuality, and want to try to maintain it. Therefore, they try to ensure that new members will enjoy, appreciate and continue those things that make the club or group unique. If your interests or talents are compatible with a particular group and you genuinely like and feel comfortable with its members, the chances are good that they will feel the same way about you. I am only listing private groups and clubs that have a purpose beyond socializing, and which are also reasonably inexpensive to join.

BY MERIT

MENSA NATIONAL HEADQUARTERS (817) 332-2600
Fort Worth, TX

MENSA DELAWARE VALLEY (215) 765-2735 (Hotline)
Philadelphia, PA

Organizes meetings and activities for people with a high IQ. Members come from a wide range of backgrounds and careers, are nice and are very supportive of each other, even on an international basis. In appearance they encompass everything from the "Absent minded professor" look to the "Dressed for Success" look. Testing is required for members (but you can re-test several times). The meetings are open to visitors. For all ages; there are as many singles as married members. Membership is approx. $30/yr. Meets on the 2nd Friday of every month.

BY INVITATION

PHILANTHROPIC GROUPS

THE JUNIOR LEAGUE (215) 923-6777 or
Philadelphia, PA (215) 923-6999

The original female answer to the masculine "Old boy" school and business network. No matter where they move, members simply contact the local branch of the "League." They are immediately introduced to other newcomers and are put to work. Originally with a "white glove" image, it is much more down to earth these days. Still all female, to join you need to be recommended by two members. You can use "Sponsor Pool" members if you don't know anyone currently in the League. In return for the League's supportive network, its members must commit a substantial amount of volunteer time to any number of the worthwhile causes the League is involved in. New members are enrolled once a year in the spring and receive their "Provisional" training in the autumn.

COMMUNITY SERVICE CLUBS

These clubs are large international organizations with so many branches in the Delaware Valley that almost every community has one. Their main purpose is to support selected charities and local causes through fund-raising efforts by members. Members consist of motivated professional men and women who want to make a difference in the world around them. They benefit from the camaraderie, friendships and business contacts they make. The clubs offer opportunities for members to develop and refine their leadership skills outside of the office arena. They also provide a network of contacts in other cities and countries. The organizations all have similar formats for becoming a member. The local club leader will tell you when and where the meetings are held. At the meetings you will meet current members and they will meet you. If you like the group you will ask to be considered for membership. If they feel that you are compatible with their group they will invite you to join.

EXCHANGE CLUB (419) 535-3232
Headquarters in Akron, Ohio

There are many in the area; they are particularly popular in West Chester. Chapters usually meet for breakfast, lunch or dinner twice or more often monthly. They sponsor events, fund-raisers and projects.

KIWANIS INTERNATIONAL (717) 540-9300
Pennsylvania District Office
Harrisburg, PA

There are many Kiwanis clubs in the Delaware Valley and all of them meet once a week, usually to mingle and listen to a speaker on a topic of interest. Member clubs often join forces with each other for fund-raising projects or occasional joint meetings. Call the district office for information about local clubs and whom to contact. **For other areas call "Kiwanis International" in Indianapolis 1(800) 879-4769.**

THE LIONS CLUB (708) 571-LION
Main Office in Chicago, Illinois

There are 100 clubs in district 14A alone (Bucks, Delaware and Philadelphia Counties). Individual clubs meet 2 or 3 times a month. The District Governor can tell you who runs the club nearest to you. For the name and number of the current District Governor, call the Chicago number.

ROTARY CLUB (708) 866-3000
Main Headquarters, Evanston, Illinois

The many clubs in the area meet on a weekly basis. To locate your nearest club, contact the Rotary Headquarters. They will put you in touch with the local District Governor of your area.

SOROPTIMIST INTERNATIONAL (215) 732-0512
OF THE AMERICAS
Philadelphia, PA

"The world's largest classified service organization for executive and professional women." An international organization, the American Chapter has more than 50,000 members.

BY AUDITION & INVITATION

THEATRICAL

HELPFUL HINTS: There is a monthly publication titled "STAGE." It lists theatrical productions and auditions in the area (professional, semi-professional and amateur). To subscribe to "STAGE" send a $9 check to Ethel Guy, Subscr. Manager, 403 Michigan Avenue, Swarthmore, PA 19081 or call (610) 328-7223. Auditions also appear in the Philadelphia Weekly, City Paper, and Sunday "Neighbors" section of the Philadelphia Inquirer. Churches often have theater groups and most of them try to use members of their congregation for the cast and stagecrew; Jewish Community Centers often mount productions as well.

I haven't found all of the groups that exist and new ones crop up all the time. Some groups stage one production a year, others stage several; some pay part of their staff and cast but also use local volunteer performers, and some are entirely volunteer based. Since it will do you little good to contact them until they are casting a new production, your best bet is to subscribe to "Stage" or to keep a constant watch on the newspapers. Once you do become involved with *one* of these groups, you'll be a part of their network and quickly learn about *all* of the others. I have performed in Community Theater. It can be a once-a-year thrill if you work with just one group, or become a most enjoyable (but unpaid) 2nd career if you manage to join several groups. If you are intrigued but intimidated, you can still take part in a production by volunteering to work backstage. (It's unlikely you'll ever be turned down.)

Semi-Professional, Community and "Somewhere-in-between" theater groups.
Allen's Lane Theater (Philadelphia, PA)
Andalusia Community Theater Company (Andalusia, PA)
Artists Theater Association (Wilmington, DE)
The Barnstormers (Ridley Park, PA)
Big Apple Dinner Theater (Kennett Square, PA)
The Brandywiners (Kennett Square, PA)
The Bridge Players (Palmyra, NJ)
The Burlington County Footlighters (Cinnaminson, NJ)
Chapel St. Players (Newark, DE)
Cheltenham People's Theater (Cheltenham, PA)
Colonial Playhouse (Aldan, PA)
Cue & Curtain Players of Immaculata College (Frazer, PA)
The Drama Group (Philadelphia, PA)
Drama Ink (Media, PA)
The Dramateurs (Jeffersonville, PA)
Drexel Hill Players (Drexel Hill, PA)
Dutch Country Players (Lansdale, PA)
Forge Theater Company (Phoenixville, PA)
Gilbert & Sullivan Soc. of Chester County. (West Chester, PA)
Haddonfield Plays & Players (Haddonfield, NJ)
Jewish Community Center of Cherry Hill (Cherry Hill, NJ)

The King of Prussia Players (King of Prussia, PA)
Langhorne Players (Newtown, PA)
Marple Newtown Players (Newtown Square, PA)
Methacton Community Theater (Eagleville, PA)
Montgomery Theater (Souderton, PA)
Narberth Community Players (Narberth, PA)
Neshaminy Valley Music Theater (Langhorne, PA)
Phoenix Players (Springfield, PA)
Playcrafters of Skippack (Skippack, PA)
Players Club (Swarthmore, PA)
Playmasters (Bensalem, PA)
Plays and Players (Philadelphia, PA)
Ritz Theater (Oaklyn, NJ)
Salem Community Theater (Carney's Point, NJ)
Sketch Club Players (Philadelphia, PA)
Spotlighters
Stagecrafters (Philadelphia, PA)
St. Andrews Players (Drexel Hill, PA)
St. Thomas Players (Rosemont, PA)
Thespis Inc. (Gilbert & Sullivan productions) (Media, PA)
Town & Country Players (Buckingham, PA)
Village Playbox (Haddon Heights, NJ)
Village Players of Hatboro (Hatboro, PA)
Villanova Theater (Villanova, PA)
Warminster Community Theater (Warminster, PA)
West Chester & Barley Sheaf Players (Lionville, PA
Wilmington Drama League (Wilmington, DE)
Woodland Avenue Players (Philadelphia, PA)
Yardley Players (Yardley, PA)

DELAWARE VALLEY OPERA COMPANY   **(215) 424-5980**
Roxborough, PA

A repertory opera company that occupies a house in Fairmount Park. They hold out-of-door performances in the summer and do indoor events in the winter. Casting auditions are held regularly but only members may attend them. The backstage crew is mostly made up of invaluable non-singing members. Memb. approx. $15/yr.

FOOTLIGHTERS THEATER   **(610) 647-9867**
58 Main Avenue
Berwyn, PA 19312

A highly organized community theater group. They offer 5 productions a year (one is a musical) and they audition for each one.

THE PHILADELPHIA REVELS   **(610) 688-5303**
P.O. Box 8223
Radnor, PA 19087-8223

They perform just before Christmas, and at other times during the year. Performers in the Christmas show (singers, dancers, musicians, jugglers, etc.) vary with the production. However, they always need volunteers to help with hair, makeup, scenery, etc.!

ROSE VALLEY CHORUS & ORCHESTRA
P.O. Box 414
Media, PA 19063

Every year, they produce one spring musical and an autumn Gilbert & Sullivan light opera. Members audition for the chorus, lead roles and orchestra. The backstage crew is made up of non-singing members. Membership is approx. $20.

THE SAVOY COMPANY
230 South Broad Street
Philadelphia, PA 19102

"The company performs Gilbert & Sullivan light operas 4 times yearly. Members are an educated, truly nice, highly social, white-collar crowd of dedicated amateur singers and backstage workers. Membership rules require that all applicants be recommended by 2 current members of Savoy, who subsequently invite them to meet the admissions committee. Potential singing members must also attend a vocal audition. (Tenors are always needed!) But applicants who are interested in backstage work don't need to do this. <u>Highly time-demanding from February to June</u>, the group offers many activities besides rehearsals. 80% of the members are single, 60% are female, and the average age is 30. Memb. is $25/yr. but additional expenses are high."

Christopher Wright (member)
Bryn Mawr, PA

CHORAL

HELPFUL HINTS: Most choral groups seem to audition in August and January, but some will do extra auditions for likely sounding candidates. For groups in your own area, keep checking the Bulletin Board pages of the "Neighbors" section of the Sunday <u>Philadelphia Inquirer</u>. Auditions are also listed in the <u>Philadelphia Weekly</u> and <u>City Paper</u> for Philadelphia residents and in the community pages of local newspapers elsewhere.

BUCKS COUNTY CHORAL SOCIETY
P.O. Box 702
Doylestown, PA 18901

A chorus of 65 volunteers. Auditions are usually given in the summer. Performances consist of classical and contemporary choral pieces.

THE CHORAL ARTS SOCIETY OF PHILA.   (215) 545-8634
Philadelphia, PA   (Center City)

A chorus of 150 volunteers. The group performs throughout the season at churches and concert halls. Entry is by audition.

CHORAL SOCIETY OF MONTGOMERY CNTY.   (215) 641-6505
340 Dekalb Pike, Box 400
Blue Bell, PA 19422-0758

A chorus of 70 volunteers, age 16 and over. The group performs all types of music, and auditions are held twice a year.

THE MASTERWORKS CHORALE   (610) 789-6318
P.O. Box 1467
Havertown, PA 19083

Choral group of 35 volunteers that give concerts in the Havertown area. They sing light classical and folk choral pieces and audition twice a year.

MENDELSSOHN CLUB OF PHILA.   (215) 735-9922
Philadelphia, PA (Center City)

The city's oldest chorus at 117 yrs. Volunteers perform traditional and contemporary music. Auditions are usually in the summer.

THE ORPHEUS CLUB   (215) 546-6648
254 S. Van Pelt
Philadelphia, PA

An all men's club that is a social group and men's chorus (4 performances a year). One performance is done in period style costume. There are 70 singing members (all ages). The club has its own building. Membership is by audition and by personal recommendation of other members. If this sounds interesting to you, ask around and network until you meet members through other avenues. You might also join as an "associate member" (which allows you to be one of the audience).

PHILADELPHIA CHORAL ALLIANCE   (215) 563-2430
c/o Chorus America

This is an umbrella organization for a large number of choral groups, most of which are professional. They can tell you who to contact if you would like to audition for one. I have already listed their volunteer based choral groups.

THE PHILADELPHIA REVELS   (610) 688-5303
P.O. Box 8223
Radnor, PA 19087-8223

This group does performances just before Christmas, and a few other things during the year. They audition talent for the Christmas show (singers, dancers, musicians, jugglers, etc.) each year, and their needs vary with the production. But they always need volunteers to help with hair, makeup, scenery and who knows what else.

SINGING CITY   (215) 561-3930
Philadelphia, PA

Volunteers (135 of them) who give concerts for the elderly, disabled, homeless, and inner-city children, and perform with the Philadelphia Orchestra. Auditions are held in the spring and late summer.

OTHER GROUPS THAT HAVE ADVERTISED FOR SINGERS
(some of these may not require an audition)
Ambler Choral Society (Ambler, PA)
Anna Crusis Choir (a feminist choir in Philadelphia, PA)
Bucks County Singers (Newtown, PA)
Centennial Singers (Southampton, PA)
Delaware Valley Choral Society (PA)
Garden State Chorale (Moorestown, NJ)

Gratz Jewish Community College (PA)
Norristown Chorale (Norristown, PA)
Philadelphia Gay Men's Chorus (Philadelphia, PA)
Pennsylvania Pro Musica (Philadelphia, PA)
Pine Baron's Barbershop Chorus (Cherry Hill, NJ)
Philomusica Chorale (Philadelphia, PA)
Sterling Community Chorus (Haddonfield, NJ)
Sweet Adelines Chorus (I believe there are a few of these in the area)

INSTRUMENTAL

If you play a musical instrument and have toyed with the idea of playing in an orchestra that uses volunteer musicians, Community Orchestras are what you are looking for. Many of their audition ads state that they are open to amateur and semi-professional, adult or high school age musicians. Community Orchestras regularly announce auditions in newspapers (particularly in September). Buy the Sunday Philadelphia Inquirer and look for the Community Bulletin Board pages in the "Neighbors" section for auditions in your area. Announcements also appear in local area newspapers and in the Philadelphia Weekly and City Paper in Philadelphia. Alternate ways of getting in touch with these orchestras include: looking in the phone book, keeping your eyes open for brochures/flyers/posters/newspaper ads advertising their concerts, asking around to locate someone connected to them and calling local music schools for possible contacts.

The following orchestras are amateur or semi-professional:
Ambler Symphony (Ambler, PA)
Audubon Community Orchestra (Audubon, PA)
Bala Cynwyd Symphony (Bala Cynwyd, PA)
Bucks County Symphony (Doylestown, PA)
Center Philharmonic (Jewish Community Center, Trenton, NJ)
Chester County Band (Malvern, PA)
Chestnut Hill Symphony (Philadelphia, PA)
Delaware County Symphony (Newtown Square, PA)
Doctor's Orchestra (Philadelphia, PA)
Golden Eagle Community Band (Mt. Holly, NJ)
Haddonfield Symphony (Haddonfield, NJ)
Haverford College Symphony (Haverford, PA)
Immaculata College Orchestra (Frazer, PA)
Kennett Symphony (Kennett Square, PA)
Lansdowne Symphony (Lansdowne, PA)
Main Line Community Big Band (Bryn Mawr, PA)
Main Line Symphony (Valley Forge, PA)
Marple-Newtown String Ensemble (Marple-Newtown, PA)
Merion Musical Band (Lower Merion, PA)
Merion Musical Society (Lower Merion, PA)
North Penn Symphony (Lansdale, PA)
Old York Road Symphony (Abington, PA)
Olney Symphony (Philadelphia, PA)

Orchestra Society (Philadelphia, PA)
Philadelphia Chamber Music Institute (Philadelphia, PA)
Rose Valley Orchestra (Media, PA)
Rose Valley Pops (Swarthmore, PA)
South Jersey Pops Orchestra (Medford, NJ)
Symphony Club (Philadelphia, PA)
Wayne Oterie (Wayne, PA)
Warminster Symphony (Warminster, PA)

NATURE / ANIMALS / CONSERVATION / GARDENS

ANIMALS / CONSERVATION / NATURE

AUDUBON SOCIETY

The organization is dedicated to the conservation of plants and animal habitats. Walks are offered as a form of recreation and nature study (the speed is usually 2-miles per hour). In addition to the walks, the Society typically offers educational programs, a camera club, a bi-monthly magazine and free meetings.

AUDUBON SOCIETY NATIONAL OFFICE (212) 979-3000
700 Broadway
New York, NY 10003-9501

When you join the National Society your membership information is sent to the chapter closest to your area code. The local Society Chapter then adds you to their mailing list and sends you local information. However, you can always join a chapter directly, even if it is not in your area.

BUCKS COUNTY AUDUBON SOCIETY (215) 297-5880
6324 Upper York Rd.
New Hope, PA 18938

This group also runs a local nature center.

VALLEY FORGE AUDUBON SOCIETY (610) 544-4217
Box 866
Paoli, PA 19301

Monthly meetings are near Newtown Square. Information flyers and walk schedules are often dropped off at libraries in the Valley Forge vicinity.

WYNCOTE AUDUBON SOCIETY
2805 Rubicam Ave.
Willow Grove, PA 19090

They have newsletters and events in their area.

BRANDYWINE CONSERVANCY (610) 388-7601
P.O. Box 141
Chadds Ford, PA 19317

Offers free Brandywine Art Museum admission, newsletters, previews, parties, art and environmental programs. Memb. $30–$50/yr.

FRIENDS OF PHILADELPHIA PARKS   (215) 879-8159
Boelson Cottage, West River Drive
P.O. Box 12677
Philadelphia, PA 19129

An organization of park groups, individuals and families. They currently have 3,000 members and manage to combine helping the city's parks and increasing public awareness with having a lot of fun. They offer: a Hoedown dinner/dance, several parties, 10 hikes, a booth at all of the city's festive events and a massive parks clean-up once a year (9,000 volunteers turn up). Members are of all ages, from kids to age 90. Memb. $25/yr. (includes a Fairmount Park Calendar.)

OPEN LAND CONSERVANCY   (610) 647-5380
P.O. Box 1031
Paoli, PA 19301

Maintains natural areas and trails for hiking, skiing, bird-watching and nature study. Guided walks by naturalists. Members receive a newsletter and invitations to special events. Memb. $16–$25/yr.

PHILADELPHIA ZOO   (215) 243-1100 x254
Philadelphia, PA

Members can participate in a great number of special events for adults and/or children. Newsletters detail weekend classes that members can sign-up for and offer a "lottery" for members to help feed the animals (a popular activity). Workshops and trips to other zoos are offered, and there are special holiday events. (Also see the Zoobilie listing under the *Special Events/Seasonal Events* category). Memb. $35–$60/yr.

SCHUYLKILL RIVER GREENWAY ASSOC.   (610) 372-3916
960 Old Mill Road
Wyomissing, PA 19610

Quarterly newsletter, field trips, canoe floats, lectures, and an annual dinner. Memb. $20–$30/yr.

Also, in the <u>Sports</u> category, see "Appalachian Mountain Club" (under <u>All Variety of Sports</u>) and " Sierra Club" (under Hiking).

GARDENING:

HELPFUL HINTS: There are specialist interest groups for everything from Bonsai to Orchid to Rhododendron growers. The PA Horticultural Soc. can probably help you locate such groups. Also check newspapers.

DEL. VALLEY HOBBY GREENHOUSE ASSOC. (610) 446-2160
229 Ellis Rd.
Havertown PA 19083

Local chapter of a non-profit organization of plant and flower growers. Members receive newsletters and attend meetings, field trips and workshops. Memb. $10.50/yr.

PENNSYLVANIA HORTICULTURAL SOCIETY   (215) 625-8250
325 Walnut Street
Philadelphia, PA 19106-2777

"For people who want to share or increase their horticultural/gardening knowledge. Offers seminars, workshops, a library, field trips (locally and abroad) and more. Members are of all ages with a greater % being female. There are several events monthly. Memb $40/$50 yr. You can also subscribe to their newsletter."

Sheila Akers (member)
Plymouth Meeting, PA

PHILANTHROPIC GROUPS

HELPFUL HINTS: These groups raise funds for special purposes. Some are organizations that you actually pay a membership fee to join (which is partly how the group supports its activities). Some of them require volunteer time from you; some of them simply offer you the opportunity to attend special events which only members and sponsors are invited to.

ABRAXAS FOUNDATION   (215) 223-8437
Philadelphia, PA

"Raises funds for children's charities through upscale parties, celebrity auctions and concerts. Businesses often become involved, and events are well attended by singles and couples of all ages, though the average age range is 30–40. Just call and ask to be on their mailing list."

Mary Maki (event attendee)
Philadelphia, PA

THE SPECIAL OLYMPICS, PHILADELPHIA   (215) 351-7224

A very flexible organization; volunteers can be coaches, site managers, buddies, or help with fund raising, special events, marketing or just about anything. Volunteers also socialize as a group and do a lot of outings, parties and events on their own.

VARIETY CLUB HEADQUARTERS   (215) 735-0803
Philadelphia, PA

Originated in 1935 by people in show business; they sponsor disabled children's activities through social and fundraising events (often held at their own club facility), and a telethon. 600 members. **Young Adults Variety Club members** are approx. 18–34 and **Regular members** are of all ages. Call for current membership fee information.

POLITICAL INTEREST

THE DEMOCRATIC & REPUBLICAN PARTIES

If you would like to be involved in the social end of politics (as opposed to simply receiving flyers in the mail), look in your local phone book for the "Republican Committee" or "Democratic Committee" of the County or Municipality you live in. Call, speak to the "Leader," explain your interest and ask to be notified when there are any events such as dinners or cocktail parties going on. Of course, you can also volunteer to campaign for a candidate you believe in. You might have noticed that campaigners are big on having a celebration when their candidate wins.

THE YOUNG DEMOCRATS & YOUNG REPUBLICANS ORGANIZATIONS

These are sub-groups of the Democratic and Republican parties. Their purpose is to inform and interest young people (age 18–39) in politics. They are often very social and offer fund-raising, educational and political events. Counties and municipalities often have their own committees and Young Members groups. To contact your local group call your local "Republican" or "Democratic" committee and say that you would like to contact the chairperson of their "Young" members group.

FOREIGN POLICY RESEARCH INST.   (215) 382-0685
Philadelphia, PA

Gives seminars on political subjects and has a library among many other things. Price of events varies.

LEAGUE OF WOMEN VOTERS, State Chapter   (717) 234-1576
226 Forster Street   1(800) 692-7281
Harrisburg, PA   17102-3220

Philadelphia Chapter Office   (215) 977-9488

Sponsors debates, lobbies for issues, backs selected candidates and helps on election day. Call to ask about chapters that meet in your area. If all else fails, try calling the State Office in Harrisburg.

NATIONAL ORGANIZATION FOR WOMEN
Pennsylvania State Chapter Office   (215) 351-5334
Philadelphia, PA
New Jersey State Chapter Office   (609) 393-0156
Trenton, NJ

"NOW" is the largest civil rights organization for women in the country. Call the State office for local chapter phone numbers.

WORLD AFFAIRS COUNCIL OF PHILADELPHIA (215) 922-2900
Philadelphia, PA

Organizes year-round dinners, luncheons, meetings and lectures with all sorts of extremely interesting panels and speakers. Their newsletter is bi-monthly. Membership is $ 35–50/yr. They also offer group tours of foreign countries.

SINGLES AND SOCIAL GROUPS

LADIES

Some women realize that in the current era they are expected to put as much effort into striking up first time conversations as men do. If you approach a fellow, work favorite interests or activities into the conversation early on and see how he reacts. If he is truly interested, you should be able to maintain his attention without much effort. If his attentions wander, he is probably not interested, probably doesn't have much in common with you and you'd be better off moving on to talk to other people.

Also, I cannot emphasize enough how important the image you present is in attracting the type of person you want to attract. For example: If you want to attract a preppy type, then dress in preppy style; if you like corporate types, dress conservatively, and so forth.

If you go to a dance with girlfriends, take turns splitting off from the group. Wander around the crowd pretending to be looking for a friend. It means you're accessible to talk to, but can escape if approached by an unappealing admirer. It's daunting for a man to approach a female when she's with friends; he's probably going to have to talk to them as well.

Lastly, you can always take the initiative and ask a guy to dance, especially if you see him lingering at the edge of the dance floor.

GENTLEMEN

Yes, I know; it isn't easy for you either. I suggest that if you have a hard time striking up conversations or dancing, then do other singles or group activities besides dancing. Or, you may have noticed by now that women who would like to be asked to dance hang out on the edges of the dance floor. If you can dance but are shy, you might as well do the same thing and maybe YOU'LL be asked to dance.

The advice I gave women about "style" of dress goes for you, too. In addition, the biggest mistake a man can ever make is to wear Polyester clothing, since 80% of the female population absolutely hates it. The biggest put-down a woman can make is to say, "He was wearing POLYESTER!" (Her girlfriends will all cringe in sympathy.)

My next advice is to mention activities you enjoy as soon as possible when conversing with a female. Ask what interests or activities she is involved in. If you share interests, your conversation will become much easier. If you don't, you'll know you are barking up the wrong tree.

When one of my girlfriends first met her husband she would not have given him the time of day except for the fact that he kept mentioning all sorts of activities he enjoyed. They were all things she liked to do too. So she agreed to do activities together with him—as friends. Six months later they were madly in love.

GROUPS

HELPFUL HINTS: These groups are based around social events for singles, *although some allow non-singles* to participate as well. Some people love singles groups because everyone is available and looking for a mate. Indeed, the odds in favor of meeting single people to date are greater this way. However, other people feel pressured this way and prefer to be less obvious about their goals. My advice is to try some singles groups before you *let* yourself decide how you feel.

Crowded events tend to break down barriers among strangers. When you are chin to chin with people, it's hard to maintain formalities. Turn your body to face them and you'll find yourself drawn into conversations with people or groups around you. I have used this technique myself.

TIPS ON SPECIFIC GROUPS

At **Catholic singles groups** don't be startled if total strangers introduce themselves to you and then quickly ask if you are able to legally marry within the church or not. **Full Figured groups** often have slender members who like to date full figured people. **Church based groups** are not always religious (sometimes they just use the space), so if it matters ask! **Parent Organizations** sometimes have dances open to non-parents.

AMPLE AWAKENINGS (215) 602-2064 (Hotline)
P.O. Box 2231 (609) 877-9116 (Hotline)
Cinnaminson, NJ 08077

"A social club for big beautiful people and their admirers." 125 Members. Memb. $15/yr. The newsletter includes personal ads, events and articles.

ART LOVERS EXCHANGE (215) 638-9866
P.O. Box 265
Bensalem, PA 19020-0265

Their newsletter contains personal ad/profiles of members (made up of art lovers and artists). Occasionally they also offer events/gatherings.

BETH EL JEWISH SINGLES (609) 461-1832
Cherry Hill, NJ

Jewish singles group (ages 35–55). They meet Tuesdays for socializing and refreshments. They also offer parties, picnics and day trips. In future they may be adding a group for older singles.

B'NAI B'RITH SINGLES UNIT (215) 751-1485
Cherry Hill, NJ 08002

The unit coordinates social and cultural activities, as well as religious events, for Jewish singles (age 28–47) in the Philadelphia area.

CATHOLIC ALUMNI CLUB OF PHILADELPHIA (215) 956-0138
P.O. Box 53287
Philadelphia, PA 19105

For single professionals, age 21+. They offer events, dances, charitable and social activities. Memb. $30/yr. Lou Fanti is the contact person.

CHRISTIAN POWERSOURCE   (609) 582-0222
FOR SINGLE ADULTS
Gloucester County Community Church
Pitman, NJ

A singles ministry and interdenominational group. They offer social events, volleyball and religious theme discussions. Members are of all ages and backgrounds. They offer free weekly volleyball and a discussion.

COMMUNITY SINGLES   (215) 822-1972
of Our Lady of Good Counsel   (215) 563-6382
P.O. Box 991
Southhampton, PA 18966

A non-denominational singles group with 7–10 events each month. They offer a newsletter, picnics, events, dinners, dances, sports, movies, holiday parties, etc. Interested members can also meet for mass on the 2nd Sunday monthly. Memb. $18/yr. Average age 25–38.

CONNECTIONS   (609) 667-3618
Unitarian Universalist Church   (609) 667-7688 (Hotline)
Cherry Hill, NJ

A non-sectarian singles discussion-and-dance group for people age 30–50. They offer socials, special interest groups and weekly dance/discussion program with buffet. You will pay a door fee.

EPSILON NEW   (215) 637-7548
St. Katherines
Philadelphia, PA (North Philadelphia)

A club for Catholic singles age 21–35. They meet the 1st Tues. monthly.

EVENTS AND SEASONAL LOCATIONS FOR SINGLES
Read the *Special Events/ Seasonal Events* section at the end of this book.

FELLOWSHIP OF CATHOLIC ADULTS   (215) 552-8732 (Hotline)
P.O. Box 303
Bala Cynwyd, PA 19004

Offers opportunities for single, professional, college-educated Catholics, age 24–40, to meet other single Catholics. They meet once a month and sponsor social, cultural, sporting and community service events.

50 PLUSERS   (215) 947-8200
Gloria Dei Lutheran Church
Huntingdon Valley, PA

Singles and couples over 50 gather for travel, dinner theater, picnics and socializing. 1st and 3rd Wed. and 2nd Fri. of each month. Memb. $5/yr.

FILMBILL RENDEZVOUS
46 North Front Street
Philadelphia, PA 19106

Single movie lovers meet every other Sun. for a film viewing at the Ritz, and discussion afterwards at a nearby restaurant. For more information send $5 with your name and address.

FREEWHEELERS
P.O. Box 392
Cherry Hill, NJ 08003

(609) 863-1526
(609) 346-0204

A single-parent camping club that camps out one weekend each month between March and Oct. They also meet once a month to plan the trips.

FRIENDLY SINGLES 50-PLUS
Berlin, NJ

(609) 767-1762

Adults over 50 who are single, divorced, widowed or separated. Social and dance every Fri., 8 pm–12 am, at the Berlin VFW on Chestnut Street.

GARDEN STATE DISCOVERY MUSEUM
Cherry Hill, NJ

(609) 424-1233

Single parents and their kids meet each other one evening a month for "Single and Together." The kids run amok and everyone has a good time.

GERSHMAN YM & YWHA
Philadelphia, PA   (Center City)

(215) 545-4400 x247

This is the Young Men and Young Women's Hebrew Association. They offer instruction in everything from social dance to volleyball and have many singles events. (Check the Jewish Exponent for listings.)
They sponsor the "JASS" Singles Hotline (see below):

JEWISH ASSOC. OF SINGLES SERV. ("JASS")   (215) 545-6466 (Hotline)
A 24-hr. listing of Jewish singles events in the Greater Delaware Valley.

GLORIA DEI SINGLES
Gloria Dei Lutheran Church
Huntingdon Valley, PA

(215) 947-8200

This is a non-sectarian singles group that meets twice a month.

HADDONFIELD SINGLES MINISTRY
Haddonfield, NJ

(609) 429-0403

Offers activities at United Methodist Church. Ask for Vivian Rodeffer.

HERPES SOCIAL SOLUTIONS
P.O. Box 1001
New Castle, DE 19720

(302) 425-4027 (Hotline)

Singles with herpes. Founded by a couple who met through a similar group. They offer monthly dances/outdoor activities in Wilmington (may add Philadelphia soon). Their newsletter has personal ads. Memb. $25/yr.

HOSEA, St. Patricks Church
Philadelphia, PA

(610) 539-3749

Catholic singles group that meets monthly for mass and socializing.

H.U.G.S.
Philadelphia, PA

(215) 557-0142 (General Info.)
1-800-611-0648 (Hotline Info.)

Weekly discussion group for singles of all ages. They cover a new topic each week, and the leader (Charlotte Miller) offers suggestions, ideas and tips. Participants turn up whenever they can and pay a $5 door fee. The 1(800) number explains a 1(900) info. line she runs. The 1(900) line features weekly info. on places to go, singles things to do, tips and ideas.

JEWISH COMMUNITY CENTERS
Kaiserman Branch (City Line Ave.)   (610) 896-7770
Klein Branch (NE Philadelphia)   (215) 698-7300
Southern New Jersey (Cherry Hill)   (609) 662-8800
Wilmington, DE   (302) 478-5660

These JCCs have all sorts of activities and clubs and almost all of them run very active singles groups for younger and older singles.

JEWISH PROFESSIONAL & BUSINESS SINGLES
P.O. Box 1355   (215) 752-2179
Bensalem, PA 19020

For singles age 35+ (not all are Jewish). They offer dances, parties and weekend trips. No membership fee. Based in lower Bucks County, their events take place all over the Delaware Valley. Send a stamped, self-addressed envelope to receive an events schedule.

JEWISH SINGLE PARENT NETWORK
P.O. Box 15
Wynnewood, PA 19096

A social group that meets several times a month (both with and without children). They experiment with various activities. Membership is $25/yr. Their goal is to create a network of supportive friends.

MATE-SEARCH INTERNATIONAL'S DATABANK
2024 Stone Ridge Lane
Villanova, PA 19085

This is the databank of a matchmaker I know; (see "About Personal Ads and Dating Services" under *Other Resources*). If you send 2 photos (one full-length, one headshot), a resume and bio, you can be in it. It's free!

MORE-TO-LOVE   (215) 928-5095 (Hotline)
45 East City Line Ave., Suite 453
Bala Cynwyd, PA 19004

"A social group for full figured singles and couples and those who love them." Holds regular dances in the Philadelphia area. No memb. fee.

MPC SINGLES 21+   (215) 295-4191
Morrisville Presbyterian Church
Morrisville, PA

Age range is 21 to around 45. They have monthly meetings. Events include movies, restaurants, theaters, museums, parties and day trips.

N.A.A.F.A   (215) 879-8588 (tape)
National Association to Advance Fat Acceptance
Horsham, PA

A branch of a national organization. This group offers social events, as well as a newsletter and support groups. Many of the members are singles. Memb. approx. $10/yr.

NATURE WALKS FOR ADULT SINGLES   (215) 345-7860
Peace Valley Nature Center
Doylestown, PA

Free guided nature walks. Call for schedule of singles walks (year-round).

NETWORK OF CHURCH OF THE SAVIOR   (610) 964-8906
Wayne, PA

This huge congregation of nice, good looking, clean-cut people has many singles activities. However, they are pretty gung-ho about their religious activities, so you will need to be serious too.

NORTHEAST JEWISH COMMUNITY SINGLES   (215) 728-7361

Singles age 35–55. Daytrips, movies, walks, museums, parties, nightclubs and temple service visits. $10/yr. memb. for the activity calendar.

NORTHEAST SINGLES CLUB   (215) 742-2363

For single people age 40+. Approx. 100 members. Memb. $10/yr.

OUTDOOR SINGLES   (215) 672-2706 (Hotline)
P.O. Box 411
Horsham, PA   19044

They offer evening walks in various locations, weekend "Hike or Bike" activities, meetings and Bridge games. Send $9 for an "Events Calendar."

PARENTS WITHOUT PARTNERS   (312) 644-6610
National Headquarters, Chicago, Ill

Has many activities for single parents and their children. Branches hold weekly dances (occasionally open to the public and non-parents). Memb. approx. $25/yr. Prospective members attend an orientation meeting. At dances, a favorite ice-breaker is, "So tell me about your children."
The Groups are called:
"**Burlington**," NJ 1(800) 624-1776 (Ans. Service)
"**BuxMont**" in Hatfield, PA (215) 752-1250 (Hotline)
"**Cherry Hill**," NJ (609) 435-3537 (Ans. machine)
"**Chester County**" in West Chester, PA (610) 383-9830 (Hotline)
"**Del Co**" in Springfield, PA (610) 328-1855 (Hotline)
"**Northeast**" Philadelphia, PA (215) 332-0622 (Hotline)
"**South Philadelphia**," PA. Ask headquarters for current contact info.
"**Valley Forge**" in Jeffersonville, PA (610) 688-4829 (Hotline)
"**Wilmington**," DE (302) 762-8272 (Hotline).

PROFESSIONAL & BUSINESS SINGLES NETWORK ("P.B.S.N.")
Box 404   (610) 353-4624
Paoli, PA   19301

Huge group with tennis parties, dances, book-discussions and more. The people attending different events can vary greatly; so try a *range* of events and get there *early* to meet people as they arrive. Non-members can attend and anyone can be on the mailing list. Memb. $50/yr. Events are all over the Delaware Valley. **Information lines: In PA** call (610) 359-9733 or 353-5544; **in NJ** call (609) 751-1002. For event info. press 4, for directions & weather update press 5, for organization description press 6.

SINGLES MINISTRIES (IN GENERAL)

Supported by churches, they offer anything from singles bible study to social groups. To locate one, ask friends, check papers, or call churches. The Christian Church Support Guide (a free magazine) lists several in Bucks and Montgomery County. To order, call 1(800) 798-7023.

SPECIAL INTEREST PERSONALS

These are described under "About Personal Ads and Dating Services" in the *Other Resources* section of this book.

ST. DOROTHY'S SINGLES GROUP   (215) 602-2828 (Hotline)
Drexel Hill, PA

A very active group of singles, age 20–40's. They have monthly meetings as well as dinners, brunches, movie outings, dance and holiday parties.

ST. PETER'S YOUNG ADULTS   (609) 663-3759
St. Peter's Roman Catholic Church
Merchantville, NJ

Catholic singles club for age 20–40+. They have dances and other activities. Meets the 1st Friday of each month. Memb. $13/yr.

SELECT SINGLES   (610) 527-4642
Box 358
Villanova, PA

"For Baby Boomer Professionals. Monthly upscale private parties. No membership fees. You must call or write for a qualification form."

SIERRA CLUB SINGLES

Part of the Sierra Club (see under Hiking in the Sports category). They hike once a month, have a meal afterwards and do other things too.

SINGLE BOOKLOVERS   (610) 358-5049
P.O. Box 117
Gradyville, PA 19039

They have dinners 1–3 times a year, but are mostly newsletter based.

THE SINGLE GOURMET   (215) 732-0260
1903 Walnut Street, Box 520   (215) 732-2008 Fax
Philadelphia, PA 19103

Members dine at various restaurants and choose "from a variety of monthly events." Members also travel to other towns.

SINGLE PARENTS SOCIETY   (215) 928-9443
Regional Office for PA and NJ   (609) 582-9808

Activities and weekly dances for single parents of all ages. Memb. $25/yr. Non-members are welcomed but must be widowed/divorced/separated. The regional office has info. about local groups and whom to call. **Groups are in:** Bucks County (Levittown, PA), Delaware County (Manoa, PA), Philadelphia (South Philly), Burlington County (Pennsauken, NJ), Cumberland County (Vineland, NJ), Gloucester County (Clayton, NJ), the Jersey Shore (Sommers Pt., NJ). **There are more: call to ask for info!**

SINGLE SOILMATES   (801) 392-0115
P.O. Box 9153
Ogden, Utah 84409

A local group may start; call for contacts. They offer a newsletter with personal ads stating interests (flowers, vegetables, organic). $30/yr. memb.

SINGLE VEGETARIANS   (609) 767-8807
c/o Vegetarian Society of S. Jersey   (609) 985-1912

Singles dine and enjoy other activites around Philly and S. Jersey. They are experimenting with events. 100 members (and still growing). See "Vegetarian Soc. of S. Jersey" (listed under Life Interest Miscellaneous).

SINGLES INTERDENOMINATIONAL   (302) 798-9690
Wilmington, DE

A singles group that meets on Fridays for dinner at various restaurants in the Newark/Wilmington area. They also have movie outings, Pot Luck dinners, card parties, game nights and other events. Memb. $8/yr.

SINGLES OVER 30   (609) 784-8501 (Voice Mail)
St. Andrew the Apostle   (609) 753-2633
Giboro, NJ

A non-denominational group. This is a very low-pressure group that emphasizes companionship. They have many "newly single" singles. Main meetings are the 2nd Fri. monthly. They also have parties, outings, breakfasts, dinners, holiday outings. Avg. age is 43. Door fee is usually $7–$10. Membership is free.

THE SINGLES SCENE   (215) 242-9250
Unitarian Universalist Church
Philadelphia, PA (Mt. Airy)

Three-phase programs every Sat. (7:30 pm–12:00 am). They start with socializing, then a discussion/workshop, and end with a dance/party.

THE SINGLES SET   (215) 938-0978 (Hotline)
Philadelphia, PA and Hopewell, NJ

"A social organization for single people." They offer ballroom dancing in the Northeast on Wednesdays, Willow Grove on Fridays, and Sundays in NJ. If asked, they will send you a newsletter.

SOUTH JERSEY SINGLE PROFESSIONALS   (609) 429-4553
38 West Azalea Lane
Mount Laurel, NJ 08054

An "Activities club" for singles 20–30. They have monthly "Planning meetings" on the 2nd Thurs. of each month, in Voorhees, NJ.; (visitors are always welcome). Their activities include: trips, parties, movies, happy hour gatherings, hikes, bike rides and more.

THE TAIL WAGGERS CLUB   (610) 644-2334
P.O. Box 336
Devon, PA 19333

For dog owner and dog lover singles. Members meet monthly for park outings, events and parties. Memb. $80/yr. The average age of human members is 35 yrs. and up. Dogs must behave, have shots, be healthy.

TEMPLE SINAI SINGLES FORUM   (215) 643-6510
Dresher, PA

The Temple sponsors 2 Jewish singles groups. One is for age 21–39, the other for 39+. They offer many trips, outings and activities.

TENTH PRESBYTERIAN CHURCH (215) 735-7688
Singles Ministry
Philadelphia, PA   (Center City)

City Light: teaching, music and socializing. Mostly singles. Age 20–40.
Impact : discussion group of urban topics, teaching, music and socializing. Mostly singles. Age 20–40
Prime Time: Teaching, discussion, music and socializing. Age 35 and up.

TOWER CLUB OF PHILADELPHIA (610) 848-7881
P.O. Box 7581
Philadelphia, PA 19101

Mostly singles. Activities for tall people (men over 6'2" and women over 5'10"). They have regular meetings, socials, dances and parties. Members and activities are all over the area including S. Jersey and Delaware.

TRANSITIONAL DINING CLUB "TDC" (610) 543-7075 (Hotline)

A social dining club for singles around Philadelphia. For a schedule send a stamped, self-addressed envelope to P.O. Box 238, Broomall, PA 19008.

TRI-STATE SINGLES (610) 358-4773 (Hotline)
P.O. Box 254
Media, PA 19063

Weekly dance parties for single adults 30+ in: Media, West Chester, Skippack, and Chadds Ford, PA; in Cherry Hill and Princeton, NJ.; and in Wilmington and Newark, DE.

VEGETARIAN SINGLES (215) 276-3198
c/o Vegetarians of Philadelphia

Meet for vegetarian meals in the Philly area. See "Vegetarians of Philadelphia" under <u>Life Interest Miscellaneous</u> in *Special Interest Organizations*.

VOLLEYBALL FOR SINGLES (610) 525-2821
Bryn Mawr, PA

Every Monday evening in the gym of Bryn Mawr Presbyterian Church.

WEEKENDERS (215) 946-7600
Levittown, PA

A singles group of mixed ages. Meets 2nd Saturday monthly.

WIDOWS OR WIDOWERS CLUB
Cherry Hill, NJ

This group sponsors a dance with a live band and refreshments every Sunday evening from 8–11 pm, at the American Legion Post 372, in Cherry Hill, NJ. (Moderate door fee.)

YOUNG JEWISH ADULTS OF DELAWARE (302) 478-5660
Wilmington, DE

Events, parties, sports and discussion groups for singles age 21–35. No membership fee. Meets at the Jewish Community Center.

YOUNG JEWISH LEADERSHIP COUNCIL (215) 893-5829 or
Philadelphia, PA   (Center City)   (215) 893-5852

A part of the Jewish Federation of Greater Philadelphia; this group is for young professionals age 21–40. They organize dances, events and travel. Members are mostly singles. Memb. $50/yr.

GROUPS THAT ARE SLIGHTLY FARTHER AWAY

MIXED DOUBLES FOR SINGLES   (908) 274-2019
Princeton Indoor Tennis Center
Princeton, NJ

Sandy Burns runs tennis parties the 3rd Sat. monthly, from 7 pm to midnight. 42 players at intermediate and adv. levels enjoy refreshments, companionship and 45 minute game segments. $29 per evening.

SINGLES ON SAILBOATS (S.O.S.)   (703) 406-0573 (Ans. Mach.)
P. O. Box 363   (703) 406-9724 (Fax Mach.)
Great Falls, VA   22066-0363

"Based in Annapolis, MD; this group has many members from PA, NJ and DE. In fact, they have offical local member "Reps." (You can save your more lengthy questions for them.) They offer many on-water activities between April–Oct., and monthly brunches in the winter. Open to novice sailors as well as experts, they also have holiday events and parties. Memb. $40–$65/yr. The avg. age range is 25–55."

                              Elinor Ely (former member)
                              Princton, NJ

GAY & LESBIAN SINGLES

HELPFUL HINTS: Singles groups do exist but they prefer to remain low-key. I suggest you look in the back of the <u>Philadelphia Gay News</u> or <u>Labyrinth</u> for periodic mentions of singles events or groups.

PENGUIN PLACE   (215) 732-2220
Gay & Lesbian Community Center
201 South Carmac Street
Philadelphia, PA   19107

This organization has a constant stream of events. They offer everything from Bingo for seniors to art exhibits, dances and parties. They have a cafe on site and act as a resource organization. They can tell you about singles activites they sponsor and/or other groups in the area.

SPORTS

ALL VARIETIES OF SPORTS

DEPARTMENTS OF RECREATION/DEPARTMENTS OF PARKS

Most townships and counties have one department or the other, or a combination of the two. They always offer/coordinate a vast number of activities for children and adults and often run Community Centers too. They can tell you about activities they organize and run, and help you contact groups that use their facilities or grounds. For example, the Little League usually makes arrangements with them and so they can often tell you how to get in touch with your local Little League.

My neighborhood Recreation Department sends out flyers every season. In February they offer: Day ski trips, Basketball and Softball leagues for boys and girls, Learn-to-swim lessons, Computer tots programs, Discount ski lift tickets, "Kid's Corner" (ages 4–6), Gymnastics, Karate, Recreational swimming, Men's volleyball, Co-ed volleyball and Scuba diving lessons. In summer they offer: a Playground program, a Pre-school program (age 4–6), Track-n-field, Tennis lessons, Amusement park discount tickets, Computer tots programs, Field hockey, Soccer, Concerts in the park, Morning lap swims, and an Open gym for high schoolers.

THE YM & YWCA

Originally "Young Christian Associations" for men and women, these organizations are now co-ed, with members from every religion and age group. They offer everything from swimming lessons for babies to activity oriented support groups. You will find them in the phone book.

THE YM & YWHA

Originally "Young Hebrew Associations" for men and women, they now offer completely non-sectarian activities for people of all ages along with activities for Jewish members. As a result, they are just as likely to attract a mixed crowd for volleyball as they are to offer Israeli folk dancing. They have lots of activities for children and their parents. Now a part of a much bigger organization, the YM & YWHAs in this area are also Jewish Community Centers (JCCs). You will find them listed under Jewish Community Centers in the phone book.

JEWISH COMMUNITY CENTERS (JCCs)

See the description for YM & YWHA.

LOCAL BARS THAT SPONSOR SPORTS LEAGUES

This is one you have to search for yourself. If you see a bar with a pool table or dart board, the chances are good that they have groups that compete on a regular basis. Bars also often sponsor volleyball and softball leagues. If you see anyone in a tee-shirt that promotes a particular bar along with a particular sport, the chances are good that the bar supplies the tee-shirts for the team and you've found a contact person.

APPALACHIAN MOUNTAIN CLUB   (610) 584-4408

The Del. Val. chapter offers group hikes, backpacking, rock climbing and canoeing. Climbing instruction is free; canoe lessons are inexpensive. Year-round hikes are rated by mileage and difficulty. The male/female ratio/age of participants varies with the activity. Members tend to be outdoors oriented, nature loving and extremely nice. Memb. approx $40/yr.

DYNAMIC DIVERSIONS   (215) 849-9944
P.O. Box 1775
Southeastern, PA 19399

A group that does parties, skiing, sailing, canoeing, ballooning, etc. I've been rock climbing with them and enjoyed it greatly. Attracts nice people who like dabbling in many activities better than being perfect at any one of them. Avg. age range is 25–45. Costs $6 to be on the mailing list.

THE FITNESS NETWORK   (609) 424-0312
14 Evergreen Drive
Voorhees, NJ 08043

A group of professionals (age 20's–30's) that meets the 3rd Sunday of each month, at 10 am, in front of Builders Square (Route 73) in Marlton for biking or jogging. They also play tennis. No membership fee.

MOSAIC OUTDOOR MOUNTAIN CLUB "MOMC"
P.O. Box 28591
Philadelphia, PA 19149

A club for Jewish singles, couples, and families that enjoy doing many different sports activities. Participants under 18 must be with a parent. Active year-round, they sail, hike, bike, etc. They meet monthly to plan future outings and events. Memb. $20/yr.

OUTDOOR CLUB OF SOUTH JERSEY
Box 455
Cherry Hill, NJ 08003

The full title is "The American Youth Hostels Outdoor Club of S. Jersey," but the club is popular with ALL ages. Activities include: backpacking, biking, camping, canoeing and cross-country skiing. They have only an official address. The club has so many things scheduled that a quarterly *booklet* is sent out to members! Memb./1 yr. $8 (3 yrs. $21).

PHILADELPHIA SPORTS & SOCIAL CLUB   (610) 527-6366
"PS&SC"
P.O. Box 1171
Bryn Mawr, PA 19010

A local club that is part of a national organization (19 clubs in other cities). The group has summer, fall and winter sports leagues. Depending on the season, they play Co-ed Touch Football, Co-ed Beach or Grass Volleyball, Co-ed Indoor Volleyball, Co-ed Soccer, Co-ed Softball, Floor Hockey, Men's Basketball. They have many party events and "Happy Hour" gatherings throughout the year. Technically, you could join just for the social events. Members are an attractive group of young working professionals in the 22–35 year age range (must be over 21). Memb. $30/yr. but any leagues you sign up for cost extra (cost varies per sport).

BICYCLING

HELPFUL HINTS: Group bike rides are a great way to meet people because all the riders immediately chat about the terrain with each other. All clubs use a rating system of "A" (very hard) to "D" (very easy) to let you know how difficult a ride will be. (Remember to bring a bottle of water on the ride to prevent dehydration.) More women participate in the easy rides, more men participate in the hard rides; *but in the early spring, everyone is out of condition.* Many participants are single; some couples bike together. Families bike the easiest rides. Just because someone is alone, do not assume they are unmarried; many people bike with groups because their spouse doesn't bike. Some clubs carpool to get bikes to the rides they schedule outside the city. In the city, it is possible to rent a bike. The yellow pages list rental places. Remember to ask renters what they require for a deposit. Another option is to check bulletin boards, garage sales and classified ads for bargains on used bicycles.

BICYCLE CLUB OF PHILADELPHIA   (215) 440-9983
P.O. BOX 30235
Philadelphia, PA 19103

Probably the largest club in the area. Leaders and members are nice and much more ethnically mixed than the other clubs. The club has good newsletters and offers an enormous number of rides for all levels, all year round. Annual banquet in January. Memb. $15/yr.

BICYCLE COALITION OF THE DEL. VALLEY   (215) Bic-ycle
P.O. Box 8194
Philadelphia, PA 19101

Volunteer organization promoting cycling, clubs and bike rights. Memb. $12–$35/yr. Meets the 2nd Mon. monthly in Philly (non-members welcome). Publishes the "Commuters' Bicycle Map of the Delaware Valley."

BICYCLING FEDERATION OF PENNSYLVANIA
413 Appletree Road
Camp Hill, PA 17011

A state-wide organization of clubs and individuals, the group offers a newsletter, a yearly rally, and information services.

BRANDYWINE BICYCLE CLUB
P.O. Box 3162
West Chester, PA 19381

Year-round group rides for all levels of ability and interest. 200 Members. They have no official phone number, just an official address. They have a newsletter and monthly meetings. Memb. $10-15/yr.

CENTRAL BUCKS BICYCLE CLUB   (610) 346-6823 (Hotline)
P.O. Box 295
Buckingham, PA 18912

A touring bike club for all levels, most of their rides are in Bucks and Montgomery Counties in PA., and in Mercer and Hunterton Counties in NJ. They offer a newsletter, some cross-country skiing in the winter, and some out of state trips. 450 members. Memb. $15/yr.

CYCLES BIKYLE & SCOTT-BIKYLE FLYERS (610) 525-8442
Bryn Mawr, PA

Bike rides (12–18 miles) leave from outside the store every Wednesday evening. The pace is a moderate "C." Spring through late September.

DELAWARE VALLEY AMERICAN YOUTH HOSTELS
(see listing under Hiking)

They organize inexpensive trips to other states and countries, and sell a book called "Bicycle Touring Routes Between Hostels in Eastern Pennsylvania and New Jersey." They also send Quarterly newsletters.

DELAWARE VALLEY BICYCLE CLUB (610) 449-6154
P.O. Box 274
Drexel Hill, PA 19026

They usually ride around the West Chester area (15 rides a month, 2 big tours a year). Their newsletter also lists non-club bike rides and races. 350 Members. Sports specialists often lecture at their meetings. Memb. $15/yr. Meets the 1st Monday of each month in Media, PA (non-members welcome.) Ask for a sample newsletter and try a ride with them.

DIAMOND STATE BICYCLE CLUB
P.O. Box 1729
Dover, DE 19903

Rides take place in Delaware.

MAINLY BIKES (610) 668-1616
Narberth, PA

This is a bike store in Narberth; group bike rides depart from outside the store on Tuesday and Thursday evenings.

PENNSYLVANIA BIKE CLUB (215) 885-5128
P.O. Box 987
Glenside, PA 19038

Holds regular Saturday and Sunday rides (A, B or C level), usually in Montgomery County locations. They have a regular race team and also have a mountain bike race team. Memb. $20–25/yr.

SHORE CYCLING CLUB (609) 965-4823
304 Beethoven St.
Egg Harbor, NJ 08215

Offers Sunday breakfast rides (10, 20 or 30 miles) on the 1st Sunday of each month (depart from Tuckahoe in Cape May Cnty.). Other weekends they meet up with other clubs. 175 Members. They have a newsletter, racing team, and sponsor 3 "Century" rides each year. All rides are in South Jersey. Memb. $10–$17.50/yr. ($5 extra for racers).

SOUTH JERSEY WHEELMEN (609) 863-6693 (Hotline)
P.O. Box 2705
Vineland, NJ 08360.

90 members. More family-oriented than a racing group. They have picnics, outings, parties and a newsletter. Meetings are held the 1st Wed. of each month in Vineland, NJ. Memb. $10–$13/yr.

SUBURBAN CYCLISTS UNLIMITED
P.O. Box 401
Horsham, PA 19044

In summer they ride every day of the week. (15–35 mile bike rides are held on Tues. and Thurs. from May–Sept.) Meets the 1st Thursday monthly. Rides are in Montgomery/Bucks County. They have a newsletter and hold 2 Century events per year. 500 Members. Memb. $12/yr.

WHITE CLAY BICYCLE CLUB ("W.C.B.C.")   (302) 529-7929
1124 12th Avenue
Murray Manor 2
Wilmington, DE 19808

15–20 mile rides every Wednesday in Wilmington, and hilly 55 mile rides every Sunday in Newark. However, they do additional rides all over S.E. Pennsylvania, Delaware and N.E. Maryland. Meetings are held the 1st Tuesday of every month. 500–600 members. Memb. $12–$16/yr. To try them out first, send a S.A.S.E. for a copy of their ride information.

WISSAHICKON OFF-ROAD CYCLISTS   (215) 844-7987
Philadelphia, PA   (215) 641-9822

A loose-knit group of Mountain Bikers. They maintain trails every 2nd Sat. (10 am) along the Wissahickon. Notices are posted near Valley Green Inn. Members tend to ride in unorganized groups, but you can meet them and become a part of their ride network if you help to clear trails.

Also see "Outdoors Club of South Jersey" (under All Varieties of Sports) and "Sierra Club" (under Hiking).

CANOEING

PHILADELPHIA CANOE CLUB   (215) 487-9674
Philadelphia, PA   (Roxborough)

An all-season canoe club that also enjoys kayaking, camping, related activities and social events. They have a clubhouse and newsletter. Membership is capped at 200. Potential members attend meetings, training sessions and public events. If a member of the club is willing to be your sponsor, you fill out an application form and wait to be nominated and voted in for membership. Memb. approx. $85–$95/yr.

Also see "Appalachian Mountain Club," and "Outdoors Club Of S. Jersey," (under All Varieties of Sports) . See "The Sierra Club" and "Wilmington Trail Club" (under Hiking).

FENCING

THE PHILADELPHIA FENCING CENTER   (215) 382-0293
Philadelphia, PA   (University City)

Programs are offered for various levels. Classes and individual lessons are provided for a very reasonable price.

Or call your local YMCA to see if they offer classes.

FRISBEE/ FRISBEE GOLF / DISC GOLF

Disc Golf is a 20 year old sport. Adults, families and kids all participate. There is no charge to use the courses in the area. To play, a frisbee/disc is thrown down a fairway. The final target is a pole with a basket on it. Courses are in Tinticum Park, Fairmount Park and Tyler State Park.

BUCKS CNTY. WHITE TAIL DISC GOLF CLUB   **(215) 463-2605**
Joe Mela
13063 Blakeslee Drive
Philadelphia, PA 19116

Or contact Scott Murray at (215) 946-8857. You can also call them and ask about clubs in other areas. This is one of 12 clubs in the Mid-Atlantic Disc Golf Club. They have 2 levels of membership. Serious competitive players pay $10 a month to receive a T-shirt, newsletter and assorted competition-related items. Less active members ("Honorary Members") pay $30/yr. and receive the basics. This group plays at Tinticum Park.

PHILADELPHIA AREA DISC ALLIANCE   **(215) 238-8751 (Hotline)**
Philadelphia, PA

The hotline for "PADA" announces frisbee pick-up game locations, official tournaments, adult frisbee league tryouts, information about leagues for juniors and frisbee player social events.

GOLF

HELPFUL HINTS: The world of private golf clubs is full of extremely expensive membership fees and waiting lists. The following list is of public golf course leagues and groups that are much less expensive to join. Although there are probably more of them, these are the few that I have stumbled across. Your best bet is to call public courses near you and ask if they have any leagues/groups that are open to the public. Golf equipment is not cheap but you can find *great* deals by looking at bulletin boards, garage sales, the classified ads or thrift shops. For example, I found a complete set of quite decent ladies clubs (with a Wilson bag) for $15 at a yard sale; the bag still had a "Pinehurst" tag on it. You can take lessons at local night schools in the area or even at driving ranges.

MEN'S PUBLIC GOLF COURSE GROUPS/LEAGUES:

These groups often have a waiting list. Seasons generally run from April to October. When you call, in some cases you may need to ask for the phone number of the current president of the group.

COBBS CREEK GOLF COURSE   **(215) 877-8707**
Upper Darby, PA
Has a Men's Golf Association.

ED 'PORKY' OLIVER GOLF CLUB   **(302) 571-9041**
Wilmington, DE
Has a Men's Golf Association.

FRANKLIN D. ROOSEVELT GOLF COURSE   (215) 462-8997
Philadelphia, PA
Has a Men's Golf Association.

JOHN F. BYRNE GOLF COURSE   (215) 632-8666
North East Philadelphia, PA
Has a Men's Golf Association.

JUNIATA GOLF COURSE   (215) 743-4060
Philadelphia, PA   (Kensington)
Has a Men's Golf Association.

MIDDLETOWN COUNTRY CLUB   (215) 757-6953
Langhorne, PA
Has a Men's Golf Association.

LADIES' PUBLIC GOLF COURSE GROUPS/LEAGUES:

These are probably just a few of the independent women's golf groups that are attached to public golf courses in the area. You might want to call the public courses around you and see if they have one. Membership is usually less than $30/yr. and leagues are usually open to any female who is interested, anytime during the season. Some of them have teams which compete against other local ladies' groups. Seasons run from April to October. When you call, in some cases you may need to ask for the phone number of the current president of the group.

COBBS CREEK GOLF COURSE   (215) 877-8707
Upper Darby, PA
Has a Women's Monday Evening League.

ED 'PORKY' OLIVER GOLF CLUB   (302) 571-9041
Wilmington, DE
Has a Women's Golf League.

MIDDLETOWN COUNTRY CLUB   (215) 757-6953
Langhorne, PA
Has a Women's Golf Association.

VALLEY FORGE GOLF CLUB   (610) 337-1776
Valley Forge, PA
Has a Ladies Golf League. This club has 9 holer and 18 holer members. Handicaps are given to members who play either one.

EXECUTIVE WOMEN'S GOLF LEAGUE (407) 471-1477
1401 Forum Way, Suite 100
West Palm Beach, FL 33401

Local Contact Person: Donna Henshaw (610) 363-0966

"A national organization with many branches. The Philadelphia league meets weekly, after work, for 9 holes of golf, socializing and networking. The current location has been Springfield, PA but that can change. Once a month, on weekends, there is a tournament. I have found it to be a valuable business resource, as well as a way to get out on the course on a regular basis. For obvious reasons the local league goes into hiatus in winter, but since the organization is national, I have the ability to travel and play with branches in other parts of the country. When you join the national organization, you are assigned to the local league, which then gives you an official PGA handicap. Abilities of the members vary greatly. The $60/yr. memb. fee includes both national and local organizations."

Pat Sidders (member)
Lafayette Hill, PA

HANDICAPPED / PHYSICALLY DISABLED ATHLETICS

See listing at the end of the <u>Sports</u> section.

HIKING

HELPFUL HINTS: Non-members can initially participate in group hikes, so call for a newsletter and try them out first. Hikes that involve car pooling sometimes have a small fee. Make sure you pack lunch and plenty of WATER!!! All hikes are predetermined, have an exact mileage, and are often rated on a Class 1(easy) to Class 4 (most difficult) scale. In general, hiking attracts educated, intelligent people with a strong love of nature (usually non-materialistic). Conversations start naturally as you fall in step with various participants during the hike and sit for lunch halfway through the hike. Although hiking boots are helpful (and waterproof ones necessary in rain or snow) many people wear thick soled running shoes. You need a thick sole for walking on rocks, good ankle support for uneven surfaces, and socks that won't give you blisters.

BATONA (215) 335-3055
(BAck TO NAture hiking club of Philadelphia)
Allen Britton
6651 Eastwood Street
Philadelphia, PA 19149-2331

I noticed no difference, but rumor says that members of Batona are older than members of other hiking clubs. I find this hard to believe; they offer 30-mile endurance hikes twice yearly with an 18-miler the week before. Most clubs hike year round, but Batona does it rain, sleet or snow, with pride! They offer Friday night "Moonlight Hikes," cross-country ski trips, holiday hikes and a yearly banquet. The $2/yr. membership fee pays for a twice-yearly hike schedule newsletter. Send a check to Allen Britton.

CHESTER COUNTY TRAIL CLUB (610) 459-3203
P.O. Box 1236
West Chester, PA 19380

More than 120 hikes yearly, in various locations. The $6/yr. membership fee entitles you to the hike schedule newsletter.

DEL. VALLEY AMERICAN YOUTH HOSTELS (215) 925-6004
624 South 3rd St.
Philadelphia, PA 19147

For youths AND ADULTS OF ALL AGES. Besides hiking, they organize skiing, sailing, biking, canoeing, backpacking and trips. They also provide access to their extensive network of accommodations across the U.S. Memb. $10–$35/yr. depending on your age.

HORSE-SHOE TRAIL CLUB
509 Cheltena Ave.
Jenkintown, PA 19046

Membership is $10–$15/yr. Has several hikes a month and a newsletter.

LIBERTY BELL WANDERERS (215) 343-6105
1076 Connemara Circle
Warrington Circle, PA 18976

A "Volksmarch" club that participates in, and hosts, 10K (6.2 mile) hikes. Trails are marked and hikers hike at their own pace but check in upon arrival and departure. Members can earn pins and badges. For all ages. Part of an international organization; the sport began in Germany.

PHILADELPHIA TRAIL CLUB
12 Harvest Mews
Newtown, PA 18940

Offers regular hikes around the Philadelphia area. (They carpool if necessary.) Their newsletter lists gathering points. Memb. approx. $10/yr.

SIERRA CLUB, S. E. Pennsylvania Group (215) 592-4063
623 Catharine Street (215) 592-4073 (Hotline)
Philadelphia, PA 19147

Dedicated to preserving habitats of rare and endangered species. They offer hikes, bike rides, events, a singles group, newsletter and magazine. Memb. $35–$43/yr. Planning meetings are on the 3rd Wed. monthly.

SIERRA CLUB, N.J. Main Office (609) 924-3141
57 Mountain Ave.
Princeton, NJ 08540

Out of 9 groups, South Jersey is the "West Jersey Group." They have regular meetings and hikes in the Pinelands and Camden County but no official phone number. Call the Princeton office for contacts.

TAKE A HIKE CLUB / 40-Something Club (610) 275-1615
3133 Stoneycreek Rd.
Norristown, PA 19401

Most members are 40+. Weekly 5 mi. walks in Valley Forge Park and monthly 15 mi. slow pace hikes. They have a newsletter. Memb. $35/yr.

UNIVERSITY OF PENNSYLVANIA OUTDOOR CLUB
Visit the Youth/Student Activities Center on campus for details on whom to contact (club officers change yearly). With a variety of activities, this is one of the few non-private school outdoor clubs in the area. Membership is open to non-students, and many participants come from other schools.

WALKING CLUB FOR OLDER ADULTS   (610) 525-2821
Bryn Mawr Presbyterian Church
Bryn Mawr, PA

Scenic 2-mile walks in the Bryn Mawr area.

WANDERLUST HIKING CLUB   (215) 580-4847
162 West Rosemar St.
Philadelphia, PA 19120

This group hikes about 5–7 miles every Saturday, and all hikes can be reached by public transport. Free! Send a S.A.S.E to receive a schedule.

WILMINGTON TRAIL CLUB   (302) 652-6881
P.O. Box 1184
Wilmington, DE 19899

For people who like to "hike, paddle and ski." Almost 400 events yearly, most in the tri-state area. Several weekly hikes. Memb. approx. $15/yr.

Also see "Outdoor Singles" (under **Singles and Social Groups**).

HORSEBACK RIDING

SADDLE CLUB   (215) 233-0341
20 Rose Lane
Flourtown, PA 19031

"Invites experienced riders to saddle-up for trail rides in Fairmount Park. 24 members share horses and meet throughout the week to ride the park's 75 miles of bridle paths." There is a $300 initiation fee (which includes 3 lessons) plus an ongoing fee of $125 per month for the upkeep of the horses.

ORIENTEERING

DELAWARE VAL. ORIENTEERING. ASSOC.   (610)792-0502 (Hotline) or
212 Westover Drive   (609) 429-2677
Cherry Hill, N.J. 08034

A Scandinavian sport in which you learn to orient yourself in the woods using a detailed map with a compass. "Meets" are for all ages (even kids) and are highly social. Some participants approach this as a "leisurely hike" and others make it a time challenge and actually RUN through the woods. The goal is for everyone to reach several target locations, in a specific order. Everyone must carry a whistle, sign in at the start and sign out when they finish. Beginner and kid training days are offered. The Association provides maps and sells inexpensive whistles and compasses. Members receive a newsletter. Memb. $12–$26/yr.

ROCK CLIMBING

HELPFUL HINTS: Climbers go to Livezey Rock (Fairmount Park), and Ralph Stover State Park. Organized lessons usually provide equipment.

BASECAMP (215) 592-7956
Philadelphia, PA   (Center City)

A climbing equipment store with an indoor climbing wall. No reservations needed; $7 a day or $4 after 4 pm (the store is open late on Wednesdays).

PHILADELPHIA ROCK GYM (610) 666-ROPE
422 Business Center
Oaks, PA   19456 (near King of Prussia)

Large facility with instruction available. Hosts monthly meetings of the Pennsylvania Mountaineering Association (P.M.A. membership $15/yr.).

RALPH STOVER CLIMBER COALITION (908) 996-7693
#7 Sixth Street
Frenchtown, NJ   08825

The newsletter lists special events and park upkeep gatherings. $10/yr.

R.E.I. SPORTS EQUIPMENT (610) 940-0808
Conshohocken, PA

They have an indoor climbing wall—it's for testing equipment. Reservations are needed and they have special hours for kids.

ROLLER BLADING / IN-LINE SKATING

LANDSKATER IN-LINE SKATE CLUB (609) 854-7774
227 Guilford Ave.
Collingswood, NJ   08108

In-line skate club with **3 "City Skates" per week (by Philly Art Museum)** and **3 weekly clinics in Cherry Hill** (small fee). Offers monthly trips and special events. 370 Members ("5th largest in the country"). The $15–$25/yr. memb. includes: newsletters, mailings, T-shirt and more.

OMNI SPEED CLUB (609) 346-1426
Echelon Roller Rink
1140 White Horse Road
Voorhees, NJ   08043

This is a speed skating (racing) club that is active year-round. They meet to train on Mon., Wed., Sat. and Sun. every week. Beginners can join and receive training. The group travels to competitions around the country.

SKATE DAWGZ (610) 525-6688
1875 Horace Avenue
Abington, PA   19001

In-line skate club run by Wilburger Ski Shops. Offers weekly **group skates in Philly, Valley Forge and other places**. Also has a parade, skate outings for "Skate Dawgz" over 40 and lessons. $25/yr. memb.

Also see activities of the various ski clubs listed (under Snow Skiing).

ROWING / SCULLING

HELPFUL HINTS: We've all seen them out on the river but most of us don't know anything about it. "Scullers" row with an oar in each hand and go out in single, two, four or eight person boats. The college crews that we see competing are usually "Sweep rowing" (each person has one oar and a coxswain helps them keep tempo by calling the pace).

"The U.S. Rowing Society (at 4 Boat House Row) can give you general information about rowing in the area. 'Boat House Row' clubs offer sweep and sculling equipment for first time rowers (usually in a wide boat to start with). Club members are age 10–90 and are of all levels of capability. Most clubs provide all your equipment and have lockers and showers; some also store private equipment. Membership prices vary but are usually a few hundred dollars per year. Most boat houses are active before and right after work hours."

Christopher Wright (former member)
Wayne, PA

BACHELORS BARGE CLUB (215) 769-9335
Co-ed membership.

CRESCENT BOAT CLUB (215) 978-9816
Co-ed membership.

FAIRMOUNT ROWING ASSN. (215) 769-9693
Co-ed membership.

MALTA BOAT CLUB (215) 765-9363
Co-ed membership.

PENN A & C ROWING ASSN. (215) 978-9458
All male membership.

PHILADELPHIA GIRLS ROWING CLUB (215) 978-8824
All Female membership (shares with Undine Barge Club.)

UNDINE BARGE CLUB (215) 765-9244
All male membership (shares with Philadelphia Girls Rowing Club)

UNIVERSITY BARGE CLUB (215) 232-2293
Co-ed membership.

VESPER BOAT CLUB (215) 769-9615
Co-ed membership.

RUNNING / RACEWALKING / WALKING

HELPFUL HINTS: Yes, you do need good running shoes or you won't find yourself running for very long. My advice is to stay away from the big mall shops and stick with small stores that are owned by people who have been running for years themselves. Since good running shoes are expensive, it's best to get experienced advice from the very beginning.

BRANDYWINE ROAD RUNNERS CLUB   (610) 696-1931
Based in West Chester. A loosely organized group that meets regularly for races. In addition, the members run in small independent groups. Call for a newsletter, try them out and then you can join.

DELAWARE COUNTY ROAD RUNNERS   (610) 583-0610
They have regular meetings, group runs and a newsletter. 75% of the members enter at least one race a year, but it's really a fun run group and they even have a few fitness-walking members. Runs tend to be in the Collingdale, Aldan and Springfield areas. No membership fee.

FAST TRACKS   (610) 640-0331
Valley Forge, PA
A running/walking club for women. Runs/Walks are held every Saturday morning and every Wednesday evening. Meetings are the 3rd Tuesday of each month in Berwyn. Memb. $12/yr. includes newsletter.

THE HASH HOUSE HARRIERS   (610) 486-6399 (Hotline)
"An international club. Runs are loosely based on a British game called 'Hare and Hounds.' A leader (Hare) starts ahead of the runners (Hounds) and leaves a trail of flour for them to follow. The weekly 6-mile run is in all weathers, across ALL terrains, in some location in the Delaware Valley. This group prides itself on its partying attitude and non-competitiveness. 75 Members, all ages, male and female. Memb. approx. $25/yr. Runs are held on Tuesday evenings in summer and Saturday afternoons the rest of the year."
                    Ed Purdy (member)
                    Delran, NJ

MIDDLE ATLANTIC ROAD RUNNERS CLUB
P.O. Box 613
Lafayette Hill, PA   19444
A distance-running information source for S. E. Pennsylvania, S. Jersey and Delaware. Memb. $12/yr. Members receive <u>Running News</u> and information about races and team competitions.

NORTHEAST ROAD RUNNERS CLUB   (215) 535-6092
Northeast Philadelphia, PA
The most active and organized Delaware Valley Road Runners group (200 members). Their newsletter lists area races and running events. Memb. $12–$15/yr. Meets the 3rd Tuesday of each month.

VILLANOVA ATHLETIC CLUB   (610) 527-5510
Fleet Feet
Bryn Mawr, PA

A club sponsored by a running store; memb. is $25/yr. for newsletter, T-shirt, after-run refreshments and discounts. Runs are on Saturday mornings and Wednesday evenings. (The Wednesday run has post-run socializing.) There is a track workout on Tuesday evening.

Also see "Orienteering" (under Sports).

SAILING / BOATING

AMERICAN YOUTH HOSTEL SAILING CLUB   (215) 925-6004
Philadelphia, PA

For ages 25–70. Weekend and day trips in summer. No experience necessary for crew members. Call for a schedule and participation fees. You must join the main Del. Val. American Youth Hostels organization. Call the number shown and ask whom to contact for the sailing club.

LIBERTY YACHT CLUB   (215) 922-4005
Philadelphia Marine Center, PIER 19
Philadelphia, PA

Club membership is open to the public at approx. $400–$1,000/yr. Membership dues are paid in installments. As a member, if you are certified, you can telephone to sign up for one of their boats in the same way that you'd call to reserve a tennis court at a tennis club. It's like owning a boat without having to deal with its maintenance. Types of sailing offered vary from fun cruises to serious racing. 4-Day sailing courses are also offered to the general public.

PHILADELPHIA SAILING CLUB   (610) 668-1234 (Hotline)
P.O. Box 53744
Philadelphia, PA 19105 (Germantown)

No, you don't have to own a boat. They welcome novices and experienced sailors to crew groups of boats chartered by the club for trips (cost avg. $125 per person). Other activities: parties, seminars and races. They have a monthly meeting/social in Germantown. Memb. approx. $35/yr.

Also see "Singles on Sailboats" (under Singles and Social Groups) .

SNOW SKIING

HELPFUL HINTS: This is where I admit that I have partied with (and been a member of) 2 ski clubs but have yet to go on a ski club trip. Many clubs plan so many non-ski-related activities that non-skiers can enjoy them too. Meetings are usually free but parties and activities have varying attendance fees (members pay less). The male/female ratio at meetings and events is usually equal. However, since more men ski in general, the resorts tend to attract more single men than single women. **Ski club monthly meetings start in September and are mainly for socializing. Membership is rarely more than $30/yr.**

Beginners! In January, keep your eyes open for mention of the annual "National Ski Day," because that's when many resorts offer free lessons, rentals, and slope or trail tickets.

Downhill skiing is more popular, but most clubs have some trips that also allow cross-country (Nordic) skiing, and one club offers ONLY Nordic skiing. Popular ski trips fill up FAST! Clubs sell discounted lift tickets for the Poconos every fall. You can also network among members to find out about "Group ski houses." (Several singles and/or couples split the cost of renting a house at a ski resort, thereby reducing their costs while achieving instant camaraderie and easy access to evening social spots.)

Clubs often sponsor bargain sales of used or discounted equipment. But ski resorts rent very reasonably priced equipment, and beginners can get a package deal combined with a lesson. As for clothes, find out what you need and then check out thrift and consignment stores around you, or borrow from a friend. I recommend buying new thermal socks and thermal underwear (not very expensive).

Cross-country skiing is cheaper than downhill, since you do not have to buy a lift ticket. Equipment is equally rentable and reasonable. It is possible to use the same clothes for either sport, but cross-country skiers need fewer layers of clothing.

EASTERN PENNSYLVANIA SKI COUNCIL

95% of the area ski clubs belong to this organization. **Every autumn the council publishes a free magazine titled "SNOWDRIFTS"** and distributes copies to ski shops in and around Philadelphia. The magazine lists some of the ski trips planned by member clubs, and has recent updates on club telephone numbers.

TUESDAY

BLAZERS SKI CLUB (215) 829-8100 (Hotline)
P.O. Box 13052 Avg. Age Range: 30–49
Philadelphia, PA 19104

The only Afro-American ski club in Philadelphia; the Blazers are a chapter of the National Brotherhood of Skiers. Their 1st goal is to encourage black skiers; their 2nd goal is to encourage very young black skiers to aim for the Olympic Games. Regular Blazer members are age 19–70+. Junior Blazers are age 5–18. Also offers: sailing, biking, picnics, parties. **Meets** the 2nd Tuesday, monthly, **in Philadelphia, PA (Center City)**.

KING OF PRUSSIA SKI CLUB
P.O. Box 60146 Avg. Age Range: 25–50
King of Prussia, PA 19406

This is considered a sports *and* social club because they organize so many things besides skiing. The club also offers: volleyball, biking, bowling, canoeing, water-skiing, golf, in-line skating, tennis, ice-skating, dances, etc. A nice, VERY energetic, professional crowd. Approx. 400 members. Some couples and many singles. **Meets** the 3rd Tuesday, monthly, **in Bridgeport, PA**. Write and ask for a copy of the newsletter.

MAIN LINE SKI CLUB (610) 356-7807 (Hotline)
214 Vassar Circle Avg. Age Range: 30–65
Strafford, PA 19087

For all levels of ability, from non-skiers to club racing-team members. The club is equally involved with year-round tennis, and half of the 800 members joined for the tennis. They also offer bridge (year round), sailing, dances, etc. This is a mature, upscale membership of singles, couples and families. **Meets** the 2nd Tuesday, monthly, **Radnor, PA**.

NEW HOPE NORDICS (215) 725-9281
P.O. Box 52688
Philadelphia, PA 19115

For lovers of the outdoors and for cross-country skiers ("cross-country" skiing is also called "Nordic" skiing). The group often has parties. 175 Members. **Meets** the 2nd Tuesday, monthly, **in Langhorne, PA.**.

NORTH PENN SKI CLUB (610) 997-USKI (Hotline)
122 Andrew Lane Avg. Age Range: 25–40
Lansdale, PA 19446

Besides skiing, the 200 members sail, raft, golf, have picnics, horseback ride, etc. **Meets** the 2nd Tuesday, monthly, **in Montgomeryville, PA**.

PHILADELPHIA SKI CLUB (215) 379-3875 (Hotline)
100 Moredon Road Avg. Age Range: 30–60
Philadelphia, PA 19115

In the N.E. Philadelphia/Huntingdon Valley Area. Founded in 1936, this is considered a sports *and* social club with tennis, golf, sailing, bowling, biking, hiking, parties, etc. The 225 members consist of both singles and families. **Meets** the 2nd Tuesday, monthly, **in Glenside, PA**.

WEST JERSEY SKI CLUB
P.O. Box 512
Mount Laurel, PA 08054

(609) 267-7693
(609) 859-3638

A family-oriented ski club that focuses specifically on skiing. 300 Members. **Meets** the 1st Tuesday (Oct.– March), **in Mount Laurel, NJ**.

WISSAHICKON SKI CLUB
115 Wischman Avenue
Oreland, PA 19075

(215) 884-9785
Avg. Age Range: 25–65

In Conshohocken, this ski club has its own ski slope and lift (with lights for night skiing) and "Chalet" (where they have their meetings). However they don't make snow, so they depend on the local weather. The club also offers ski trips, parties, dances, biking, sailing, etc. **Meets** the 2nd Tuesday, monthly, **in Conshohocken, PA**. 220 Members. There is a one time initiation fee of approx. $45–$85, besides the yearly dues.

WEDNESDAY

ALPHORN SKI ASSOCIATION
P.O. Box 365
Lahaska, PA 18931

Skiing for all levels. Wintertime focus is skiing. Summertime activities include: picnics, bike rides and golf outings. 95 Members. **Meets** 8 pm, 1st Wednesday monthly, at Jenny's Restaurant **in Peddlers Village, PA**.

BRANDYWINE VALLEY SKI ASSOCIATION
113 West Chester Street
West Chester, PA 19380

(610) 431-3458
Avg. Age Range: 30–55

Skiing for all levels. Also offers: volleyball, sailing, rafting, dances, parties, etc. The 140 members are a mix of singles and couples.
Meets 1st Thursday and 3rd Wednesday, monthly, **in Downingtown, PA**.

BUCK RIDGE SKI CLUB
P.O. Box 179
Bala Cynwyd, PA 19004

(215) 848-5247
(610) 664-9506
Avg. Age Range 40–65

Skiing for all levels (they also do cross-country). Family oriented and very physically active. The meetings tend to draw older members, but other events attract entire families and members of younger ages. They have a lot of S. Jersey members. They also do: parties, hiking, sailing, biking, camping, golf and lots of canoeing/kayaking. They have their own lodge in Vermont, but make trips to other places as well. **Meets** the 2nd Wednesday, monthly, at the Masonic Auditorium **in Springfield, PA**.

BUCKS COUNTY SKI CLUB
P.O. Box 763
Doylestown, PA 18901

(215) 659-1435
Avg. Age Range: 30–60

Skiing for all levels. Also offers: parties, outings, biking, rafting, etc. 300 Members. **Meets** the 2nd Wednesday, monthly, **in Horsham, PA**.

BUCKS MOUNT SKI CLUB
P.O. Box 424
Levittown, PA 19056

(215) 364-4790 (Hotline)
Avg. Age Range: 25–50

Skiing for all levels. They ski in the winter and have other activities in the summer. Made up of singles, couples and families. **Meetings** are for socializing. **Meets** 1st and 3rd Wednesdays, monthly, **in Langhorne, PA.**

SOUTH JERSEY SKI CLUB
P.O. Box 8632
Cherry Hill, NJ 08002-0632

(609) 424-8706 (Hotline)
Avg. Age Range: 30–50

Skiing for all levels. The club also offers: parties, dances, softball, sailing, canoeing, rafting, weekly volleyball, hiking, etc. **Meets** the 1st and 3rd Wednesdays, monthly, **in Mount Laurel, NJ.**

WILMINGTON SKI CLUB
P.O. Box 1331
Wilmington, DE 19899

(302) 792-7070 (Hotline)
Avg. Age Range: 30–45

Skiing for all levels. Winter activities: skiing, indoor volleyball and football. Summer activities: swimming/sailing at Dewey Beach, picnics, tennis, softball and more. On Fridays, they have "Happy Hour" gatherings. 900 Members. **Meets** 2nd Wednesday, monthly, **in Wilmington, DE.**

THURSDAY

Also see Brandywine Valley Ski Association (listed under WEDNESDAY)

FALL LINE SKI CLUB
P.O. Box 1535
Cherry Hill, NJ 08034

(609) 931-4462 (Hotline)
Avg. Age Range: 25–45

Skiing for all levels. Offers: rafting, parties, sailing, etc. 1/3 of the members live in Philly. Some couples, lots of singles. Members/visitors must be over 21! The club gives a major party "The SnoBall" every September. **Meets** 1st and 3rd Thursdays, monthly, **in Mount Laurel, NJ.**

HUNTINGDON VALLEY SKI CLUB
600 Bryant Lane
Hatboro, PA 19040

(215) 675-7250
Avg. Age Range: 30–70

They have family members of several generations, which means the members range from children to 80 years of age. Focus is on skiing. Meetings are social, often with dancing. They also offer social outings (golf, tennis, picnic). **Meets** 1st and 3rd Thursdays, monthly, **in Willow Grove, PA.**

MEETING DAY VARIES

SKI CLUB OF DELAWARE VALLEY
P.O. Box 422
Drexel Hill, PA 19026

(610) 449-7297
Avg. Age Range: 20–35

The membership is young, with a mix of singles and couples. The focus is on skiing. Monthly meeting days and locations vary.

Also see "Outdoors Club of S. Jersey" (under <u>All Varieties of Sports</u>), "Batona Hiking Club" (under <u>Hiking</u>) and <u>Sports for the Handicapped</u> at end of section.

SURFING

HELPFUL HINTS: Since I know next to nothing about surfing, the best advice I can give you is to call the phone numbers below and ask them how beginners start surfing. They should be able to tell you what to start with in surfing equipment, if there is an inexpensive way to start off (such as with a used board), and the best way to find group instruction.

EASTERN SURFING ASSOCIATION
Maryland Headquarters　　　　　　　1(800) WE-SHRED
South New Jersey District Office　　　(609) 884-5277
Delaware District Office　　　　　　　(302) 227-4011

A national organization that sponsors surfing competitions and promotes environmental awareness. Membership is $12/yr. plus $2 to enter your competition division. Rather than attending meetings, the members simply gather at competitions in the area. Their newsletter gives contest dates and news updates.

SWIMMING / SCUBA DIVING

DELAWARE UNDERWATER SWIM CLUB　　(302) 792-7867
P.O. Box 5174
Marshalton Station
Wilmington, DE 19806

The largest club on the East Coast (200 members). Meets 1st Thursday, monthly, in Wilmington. Activities include: ocean diving, spear fishing, expeditions, shipwreck diving, social events, picnics. Memb. $26–$40/yr.

DOC'S DIVERS DIVE CLUB　　(215) 364-0408
275 Second Street Pike
Southampton, PA 18966

Based out of a store, this club has new management and new energy. They offer group dives and meet monthly at the store to try new skills and equipment in their own pool. They are starting a buddy system list; if you need a companion for a dive you'll simply call people on the list.

KEYSTONE DIVING ASSOCIATION　　(610) 436-0176
101 Bartram Lane
West Chester, PA 19380

Based out of store called "Duda's Diving Duds" which organizes regular club dives. They have meetings and parties.

PHILADELPHIA DEPTH CHARGERS　　(215) 438-0749
P.O. Box 182
Philadelphia, PA 19105 (Center City)

Established in 1955, the club now has some 2nd and 3rd generation members. They dive every weekend from May–October and meet socially almost every Thursday year-round. Also: parties, special events, outings and holiday celebrations. Members consist of singles and families. Memb. approx. $60/yr. They also offer diving certification courses.

WRECK RAIDERS SCUBA CLUB   (215) 245-6018
122 Monroe Avenue
Penndell, PA 19047-4058

Meets 2nd Monday, monthly, in Levittown, PA. Offers group dives, land and water sports, picnics, parties and a Scuba Olympics. Memb. $30/yr.

TABLE TENNIS

WATERFRONT TABLE TENNIS CLUB   (215) 339-1948
230 North Delaware Ave.
Philadelphia, PA 19106

For all levels. Participants can join for the day ($3), for 1 month, or 6 months at a time. This is a new and growing group. Mark Williams is the contact person.

TENNIS

HELPFUL HINTS: Group tennis lessons from places like the YMCA, Community Recreation Center, or local community night schools are the cheapest way to learn tennis. You will need to find out what handle grip size you need (or you might end up with tennis elbow very quickly). The best way to do that is to ask a salesperson at an equipment store. You can buy used racquets fairly easily (bulletin boards, newspaper ads, word of mouth, and yard sales). Or wait for tennis racquets to go on sale at local stores; it's best to research what you need first. Talk to various salespeople and tennis players to get advice.

Also see "The Main Line Ski Club" (under Snow Skiing), and "Professional Business Singles Network" under the Singles and Social Groups section of *Special Interest Organizations*.

Also read the information at the beginning of the Sports category about Recreation Centers, YM & YWCA's, YM & YWHA's and JCC's.

TENNIS PARTIES   (609) 520-0015
Princeton Indoor Tennis Center
Princeton, NJ

Yes, Princton is slightly farther away, but there are three tennis party groups so I thought it was worth mentioning. Each group has one party per month. One group is strictly for singles and is described in the Singles and Social Groups category ("Mixed Doubles for Singles"). The other two groups appear not to have titles. One is run by Barbara Drago and the other is run by Lori Watson. Call the Tennis Center for current contact phone numbers and basic information.

TRIATHLON

PENNSYLVANIA TRIATHLON CLUB
P.O. Box 21332
Lehigh Valley, PA 18002-1332

This is the only Triathlon Club currently in the area. Family membership is $25/yr. and Team membership is $80/yr. The club offers: a newsletter, magazine, July 4th Duathlon & picnic, annual Ironman party, product discounts and various events and competitions. Team members also receive official team clothing.

WATER SKIING

PORT INDIAN SKI CLUB (610) 666-5533 (clubhouse)
93 West Indian Lane (610) 326-8605
Norristown, PA 19403

All water skiers and beginners are welcome. Members include fun-skiers and competitive skiers. Members do not need to own a boat. Meets officially on the 3rd Wednesday of each month between March–October, at dusk, on the club's waterside property. The club has a yearly water show, hosts tournaments, holds clinics and has a Christmas party. Memb. approx. $70–$100/yr. with a $150 initiation fee.

WINDSURFING / BOARDSAILING

HELPFUL HINTS: I should first mention that the true name for the sport is "Boardsailing." Locally, boardsailers go to Rehoboth Bay, Dewey Beach and Lums Pond (near Newark) in Delaware, and Marsh Creek State Park in West Chester, PA. In New Jersey, they mostly go to the bays and oceans at the shore. In Maryland, they visit the Chesapeake Bay, Turkey Point or Susquehanna flats. In PA, Marsh Creek is particularly good for beginners (easy to get lessons, rent equipment, and highly social for water sports). Since beginners start with a very short board and small sail, it's best to rent while learning. Once you are ready for intermediate sized equipment you can often buy it used. This is because boardsailers who have been in the sport for awhile often decide it is time for them to move on to bigger or more specialized equipment. Ask around for group lessons or inexpensive private lessons.

DELAWARE VALLEY BOARDSAILING ASSOC. (610) 566-7112
271 Clover Circle
Media, PA 19063

"Meets on the 1st Tues. of every month, year round. They have a Christmas party and at least one summer party. Their newsletter lists races and area special events. For singles and families. Memb. approx. $20/yr."

         Murray Hadley (former member)
         Bridgeport, PA

SPORTS FOR THE PHYSICALLY HANDICAPPED

HELPFUL HINTS: You may be amazed at the number of sports in the area that are accessible to disabled athletes. I have been told of everything from golf events to skydiving for the handicapped. There are also several national organizations (Outward Bound is one) that offer wilderness trips with kayaking, camping and the like. Several of the following organizations also act as resource centers. In other words, if you have a sport you badly want to pursue, they will try to tell you where you can find it, even if they do not offer it themselves.

EASTERN AMPUTEE GOLF ASSOC.   **(610) 867-9295**
2015 Amherst Drive
Bethlehem, PA 18015

A golf league for amputees. They organize games/tournaments.

LITTLE LEAGUE CHALLENGER DIVISION
For Handicapped Youngsters

Contact your local Little League or Police Athletic League (see Index) to ask if there is a Challenger Division of the Little League in your area.

MAGEE REHABILITATION HOSPITAL   **(215) 587-3000 (Main #)**
Philadelphia, PA (Center City)   **(215) 587-3412 (Rec. Dept.)**

Magee has many wheelchair athletic programs. They also act as a resource center and will help you locate other sports in the area.

MOSS REHABILITATION HOSPITAL   **(215) 456-9900 (Main #)**
Therapeutic Recreation Department   **(215) 456-9105 (Rec. Dept.)**
Philadelphia, PA (North Philadelphia)

Offers all kinds of support groups, has a resource library and offers week long camping trips for the disabled, among other things. They are a resource center for all types of information for the disabled, and their recreation department has information about sports in the area.

PENN. ASSOC. FOR BLIND ATHLETES   **(610) 394-9740**
50 East Plumstead Ave.
Lansdowne, PA 19050

A non-profit organization founded to increase the involvement of the visually impaired in athletic activities.

PHILA. AREA HANDICAPPED SKI CLUB   **(215) 222-6277**
4318 Spruce Street
Philadelphia, PA 19104

An information and resource center for handicapped people interested in sports. The organizers run handicapped skiing activities in the Poconos (mostly at Jack Frost). The contact person is Isabelle Bohn.

ROWING PROGRAM FOR THE DISABLED   **(215) 677-3668**

The title is fairly self-explanatory. Among other things, they organize a regatta every September. Contact person is Terri Oliver.

TRAVEL / LANGUAGE / HERITAGE GROUPS

AFRO-AMERICAN HISTORICAL   **(215) 574-0380**
& CULTURAL MUSEUM
Philadelphia, PA

Lectures, workshops and entertainment programs for all ages. For holidays they offer special festive programs with music and story-telling. Their Kwaanza celebration runs from Dec. 26–Jan 4. Memb. $25/yr.

ALLIANCE FRANCAISE OF PHILADELPHIA   **(215) 735-5283**
Philadelphia, PA

Promotes the French language and culture through lectures, cultural events, language lessons, conversational lunches in French and a Bastille Day party. Memb. $40–$70/yr.

AMERICA-ITALY SOCIETY   **(215) 735-3250**
Philadelphia, PA

The Society offers language courses, cultural activities, concerts, films, seminars and receptions. Memb. approx. $35–$55/yr.

GEOGRAPHICAL SOCIETY OF PHILADELPHIA   **(215) 563-0127**
Philadelphia, PA

"Their film/lecture series (8 to 10 a year) takes place at the Academy of Music. They have a yearly banquet and offer day trips to interesting sites, theater shows, etc. Members tend to be older rather than younger. The lectures truly are very interesting and can even be hysterically funny at times. Memb. is $60/yr. plus the seat subscription price for the lecture series. (Prices vary depending on where you sit.)"

                              Stephen Chapman-Schroeder (former memb.)
                              Villanova, PA

GERMAN SOCIETY OF PENNSYLVANIA   **(215) 627-2332**
Philadelphia, PA

Founded in 1764. Offers lectures, concerts, language lessons, relaxed "Conversational Evenings," a newsletter, cultural events, an Oktoberfest, and the largest private German library in the U.S. Memb. approx. $50/yr.

INTERNATIONAL HOUSE OF PHILADELPHIA   **(215) 387-5125**
Philadelphia, PA   (University City)

A non-partisan center and residence for 450 students from 60 countries. Offers international films (new and classic), a folk life center, programs and social activities, trips and a host family program. Non-students can be members for $30–$50/yr.

SWEDISH HISTORICAL MUSEUM   **(215) 389-1776**
Philadelphia, PA   (South Philadelphia)

A museum that promotes Swedish culture and history through lectures, events, meals, weaving lessons, Swedish language lessons and holiday celebrations. (See the *Special Events/Seasonal Events* **category.) Memb. $25-$40/yr.**

VOLUNTEER / COMMUNITY SERVICE ORGANIZATIONS

BIG BROTHER-BIG SISTER
National Headquarters   (215) 567-7000
Philadelphia, PA

Philadelphia Branch   (215) 557-8600

Volunteers become a substitute brother/sister to children or teenagers from distressed families. This does not necessarily mean they live in poverty; they may simply have lost a parent through divorce or death.

COMMUNITY ACCOUNTANTS   (215) 662-0211
3508 Market Street (University City)
Philadelphia, PA

Helps small businesses with their accounting, for free. Many of the applicants are non-profit organizations; some are involved in the arts.

CONTACT PHILADELPHIA   (215) 877-9099 (9 am to 4 pm)
                                              (215) 879-4402 (Anytime)

"Delaware Valley's only hopeline for the troubled, deaf and elderly." Volunteers remain anonymous as they listen, give emotional support and assist callers with problem solving.

LITERACY COUNCILS IN THE AREA:

These are organizations that train volunteers to teach people to read and write, or help them improve their reading and writing. They will set you up with someone in your area. You will usually teach your student at a local library. Some students are learning English as a second language.

Delaware County Literacy Council   (610) 876-4811
Center for Literacy (Philadelphia Cnty)   (215) 474-1235
Chester Cnty Library Adult Literacy Program   (610) 363-0884
Bucks County, VITA Literacy Center   (215) 345-8322
Literacy Council of Norristown (Mont. Cnty)   (610) 292-8515

LEADERSHIP INC.   (215) 893-9999
Philadelphia, PA

For people with a middle or upper management background who would like to volunteer their skills. Volunteers are asked what sort of group they'd be interested in helping (the arts, ecology, education, etc.) and are trained to work with them. They are then paired up with a group that has asked for help.

PALS FOR LIFE   (610) 525-7120
14 Elliott Avenue, Suite 10
Bryn Mawr, PA 19010

Brings animals to visit nursing homes, mental health facilities, rehab. centers and homes for the handicapped. Volunteers bring their pets or help with animals borrowed from local shelters.

PHILADELPHIA CARES   (215) 602-CARE

A central clearing house for all sorts of volunteering projects. They will ask you to attend an introductory meeting.

THE VOLUNTEER ACTION COUNCIL   (215) 665-2474
Philadelphia, PA

Volunteers fill out a questionnaire that extracts their skills and interests. The volunteer is matched with an organization that needs their skills.

VOLUNTEER FIRE DEPARTMENTS

Just stop by your nearest one and ask what it's all about.

SENIOR VOLUNTEERS NEEDED

FAMILY FRIENDS   (215) 204-3196
Philadelphia, PA

"Once or twice a week, older volunteers visit families with a child that has special needs. They provide companionship and support to the child. The children in this program are lagging in some area of development but the degree can vary. A stipend is provided to cover travel and food costs. Contact Adam Brunner for more information."

                       Anne Anspach (a mother)
                       Philadelphia (Mt. Airy), PA

FOSTER GRANDPARENT PROGRAM
Philadelphia   (215) 686-9050
Media (Delaware County)   (610) 891-4455
Norristown (Montgomery County)   (610) 272-8997

Seniors (60+) provide companionship and guidance to children in hospitals and day care centers. A stipend and lunch are provided.

PHILADELPHIA BOARD OF EDUCATION.   (215) 299-7774
VOLUNTEER SERVICES
Philadelphia, PA

Senior volunteers act as teacher aides/tutors in schools near their home.

THE RETIRED SENIOR   (215) 587-3583
VOLUNTEER PROGRAM
"R.S.V.P."
Philadelphia, PA

Ask about your local branch. Volunteer assignments for people 55 and older, who want to share their skills with others in their neighborhood. Out-of-pocket expenses are reimbursed; transportation is provided.

SERVICE CORPS OF RETIRED   (215) 596-5834
EXECUTIVES
"S.C.O.R.E."
Philadelphia, PA   19104

Retired volunteers provide technical assistance to small business owners. Technically, you don't need to a senior to volunteer for this. It's just that there aren't many 30 year old retired executives around!

NOTES

NOTES

LOCAL SUPPORTIVE ORGANIZATIONS

In and Around
PHILADELPHIA

ADDICTION RELATED

HELPFUL HINTS: Dealings with any of the organizations that have "Anonymous" in their title will require some patience on your part. Since the whole point is to allow members to remain anonymous, new applicants are often simply given telephone numbers to call, but no names. If the people who answer can't help you they will pass you along to someone else by giving you more phone numbers. Basically it's a big, benevolent, underground self-help network. Most groups offer a meeting every day, in some part of the city or area. Most organizations teach a 12-step treatment approach. Since it is common for new participants to need daily support, they are encouraged to find various meetings and to go to as many of them as they can. For most organizations, I have simply listed the central office number in Philadelphia.

There are 3 ways to find support groups in your own area:
1. Call the main downtown office and ask.
2. Look in your local phone book.
3. Buy *your local* Sunday <u>Philadelphia Inquirer</u> and look at the community Bulletin Board page; the listings change to reflect the area where the paper is sold. Or look for similar listings in your local papers.

HOTLINES

Addiction Help Line   (610) 645-3610 (Hotline)
    1(800) 238-4357
Telephone counseling and referrals.

Addiction Information, Ref. & Intervention   (610) 744-9796

Alcohol Hotline   1(800) 252-6465
Nationally based, offers phone support and referrals to groups/hospitals in your area.

Contact Philadelphia   (215) 879-4402
Counseling and Crisis Intervention
For people who are distressed and in need of someone to talk to.

Crisis Intervention (mental health)   (610) 873-1000
West Chester, PA
For Chester County residents only.

Daemion House Adolescents' Crisis Line   (610) 647-1431
Does telephone counseling and then refers callers to organizations that offer counseling in their area.

First Call For Help (United Way)   (215) 568-3750
A referral information service of self-help groups in the area.

LOCAL SUPPORTIVE ORGANIZATIONS

National Institute On Drug Abuse　　　1(800) 662-HELP
Nationally based, offers telephone counseling and refers you to local organizations that can help with the problem.

Suicide & Crisis Intervention Services　　　(215) 686-4420
Philadelphia, PA

Youth Crisis Line　　　1(800) 448-4663
Nationally based, offers telephone counseling and refers you to local organizations that can help with the problem.

ALCOHOL / DRUGS / NARCOTICS

ADULT CHILDREN OF ALCOHOLICS　　　(215) 333-0444
& DYSFUNCTIONAL FAMILIES
Philadelphia, PA

For families of people addicted to alcohol.

AL-ANON FAMILY GROUPS DEL. VALLEY　　　(215) 222-5244
Philadelphia, PA

For relatives/friends of alcoholics.

AL-ASSIST　　　(215) 592-4241
Philadelphia, PA

Outpatient drug and rehabilitation. Particularly for people arrested for driving under the influence.

ALATEEN　　　(215) 222-5244
Al-anon Family Groups Del. Valley
Philadelphia, PA

For teenaged children of alcoholics.

ALCOHOLICS ANONYMOUS　　　(215) 574-6900
Central Office & Information Center
Philadelphia, PA

Call for information about local support groups.

ALCOHOLISM AND ADDICTIONS COUNCIL　　　(610) 566-8143 (Hotline)
OF DELAWARE COUNTY
Media, PA

For alcohol/drug abusers in Delaware County.

COCAINE HOTLINE (Phoenix House)　　　1(800) COCAINE

Helpline for Cocaine addicts.

NAR-ANON　　　(215) 218-2231
Philadelphia, PA

For relatives and friends of drug users.

NARCOTICS ANONYMOUS　　　(215) 934-3944
Philadelphia, PA

Support groups for people addicted to drugs/narcotics.

Page 84 **ADDICTION RELATED**

NATIONAL COUNCIL ON ALCOHOLISM   (215) 557-9311
Philadelphia, PA
Answers questions with information and referrals.

WOMEN FOR SOBRIETY   1(800) 333-1606
Philadelphia, PA   (215) 536-8026
Offers self-help groups nationally.

GAMBLING

DEBTORS ANONYMOUS   1(800) 322-1132 X 1219

GAM-ANON FAMILY SERVICES   (215) 389-3325 (Hotline)
Support groups for relatives and friends of gamblers.

GAMBLERS ANONYMOUS   (215) 468-1991 (Hotline)
Support groups for those addicted to gambling.

SMOKING

NICOTINE ANONYMOUS
I often notice meetings of this group in local newspapers that list community meetings. If you can't locate one near you, give this address a try: P.O. Box #323, Darby, PA 19023-0323, "For anyone who has a desire to quit smoking. No dues or fees. For further information send a stamped, self-addressed envelope."

SMOKENDERS   (215) 332-8813
Philadelphia, PA
For people who want to quit smoking or those who have quit and need help with maintenance.

SMOKERS ANONYMOUS   (215) 468-0932
Philadelphia, PA
For people who want to quit smoking or those who have quit and need help with maintenance.

SMOKE STOPPERS
For people who want to quit smoking or those who have quit and need help with maintenance. Smoke Stopper programs are usually offered by hospitals and are often supported by local HMO's.

WEIGHT RELATED

HELPFUL HINTS: For many people, an emotional addiction to food makes them overweight. "OverEaters Anonymous," approaches food with the same 12-step program method that Alcoholics Anonymous uses. However, there are other people who find that basic family genetics make it hard to lose weight, and I have listed support groups for them as well; (see groups included among <u>Singles and Social Groups</u> under *Special Interest Organizations*).

LOCAL SUPPORTIVE ORGANIZATIONS

AMERICAN ANOREXIA/BULIMIA ASSOC. (215) 221-1864
OF PHILADELPHIA
Call for referrals and information about local support groups.

OVEREATERS ANONYMOUS (215) 848-3191 (Hotline)
Offers self-help groups and a daily taped supportive message at (215) 848-2820.

OTHER ADDICTIONS / ALL ADDICTIONS

ADULT & FAMILY SERVICES (215)) 686-7150
Call for information and referrals to local support groups.

CO-DEPENDENTS ANONYMOUS (215) 333-7775
Philadelphia, PA
Support for co-dependent people.

C.O.R.A. (215) 342-7660
Counseling & Referral Assistance
Philadelphia, PA

COUNSELING AND SUPPORT GROUPS
Family Service of Bucks County	(215) 757-6916
Family Service of Chester County	(610) 696-4900
Family & Social Service of Delaware County	(610) 566-7540
Family Service of Montgomery County	(610) 272-1520
Family Service of Philadelphia County	(215) 875-3300
Youth & Family Services, NJ State Hotline	1(800) 331-DYFS (Hotline)
Youth & Family Services, NJ Southern Reg.	(609) 567-0010
Catholic Social Services, Philadelphia	(215) 587-3900
Catholic Family Life Bureau, South Jersey	(609) 756-7957
Episcopal Community Services, Phila. area	(215) 351-1400
Jewish Family & Children's Service, Phila. area	(215) 545-3290
Jewish Family & Children's Service, S. NJ	(609) 662-8611
Lutheran Children & Fam. Serv. of E. PA	(215) 276-7800
Samaritan Counseling Center, PA	(215) 247-6077

Many of these organizations have offices in several locations. Most offer all types of support groups, individual counseling and lend their facilities to a variety of support organizations for meetings. The religious organizations offer many things that the County Services do, but they also have groups that have religion in common. Usually, their counselors have been trained in psychology. Samaritan Counseling Center is in 8 areas, is inter-religious and doesn't discuss religion unless you do.

FAMILIES ANONYMOUS (215) 750-4824
Philadelphia, PA
Supports families of people suffering from addictions.

NATIONAL SELF-HELP CLEARING HOUSE (212) 354-8525
New York, NY
Located in Manhattan, they will try to match you up with the support group that you need, locally or nationally.

DISEASE OR INJURY RELATED

OBSESSIVE COMPULSIVE FOUNDATION (610) 525-1510
Philadelphia, PA

SEX AND LOVE ADDICTS ANONYMOUS (215) 731-9760
Philadelphia, PA

THE STARTING POINT, INC. (609) 854-3155
Westmont, NJ

"A non-profit education and referral center specializing in the area of dependencies." They coordinate many 12-step addiction programs.

WOMEN IN TRANSITION (215) 751-1111
Philadelphia, PA

Support groups and referrals for females and family members.

DISEASE OR INJURY RELATED

HOTLINES

AIDS Hotline (Philadelphia) 1(800) 662-6080
AIDS Hotline (National) 1(800) 342-2437

Association for Speech & Hearing 1(800) 638-8255

Cancer Information 1(800) 4-CANCER
The National Cancer Institute, affiliated with cancer centers across the country.

First Call For Help (United Way) (215) 568-3750
A referral information service of self-help groups in the area.

Medicare Hotline 1(800) 382-1274

National Alliance for the Mentally Ill 1(800) 950-NAMI
Call to learn more about mental illness, or to find help if someone you know suffers from mental illness.

National Council on Aging 1(800) 424-9046

National Health Information Center 1(800) 336-4797
Provided by a branch of the U.S. Public Health Service; they will refer you to organizations for specific diseases.

National VD Hotline 1(800) 227-8922
The American Social Health Association.

Organ Donor Card Request Hotline 1(800) 243-6667

Planetree Health Resource Center (415) 923-3680
Information-by-mail service for a $95 fee. Researchers can compile the latest medical literature on a disease and mail it to you.

State Health Hotline 1(800) 692-7254

LOCAL SUPPORTIVE ORGANIZATIONS

SUPPORT GROUPS

HELPFUL HINTS: These are main branch numbers or the only phone number or address that I have come across. You can call and ask if there is a branch or group near to you. Your other option is to buy the Sunday Philadelphia Inquirer and look for the community "Bulletin Board" page. It will list groups that meet in your area. Or buy your local community newspaper; it will probably have something similar. Remember that support groups for friends, family and caretakers also exist!

AIDS RELATED
AIDS & Cancer Research Foundation   1(800) 373-4572
AIDS Information Network, Phila., PA   (215) 922-5120

ALS
ALS Association, Phila., PA   (215) 643-5434
Monthly support groups. ALS is also called Lou Gehrig's disease.

ALZHEIMER'S DISEASE
National Alzheimer's Association, Phila., PA   1(800) 272-3900 (Hotline)
Alzheimer's Association of Greater Phila., PA (215) 568-6430
Will refer you to local support groups for caregivers, family and friends.

ARTHRITIS
Arthritis Foundation   (215) 665-9200
Philadelphia, PA   1(800) 355-9040

ASTHMA & ALLERY RELATED
Asthma & Allergy Foundation   (610) 630-8050
S.E. Pennsylvania Chapter

AUTISM
National Assoc. for Autistic Children, Phila. (215) 878-3400

BURN SURVIVORS
Phoenix Society   (215) 946-2876
Offers self-help groups, peer counseling, group meetings.

CANCER RELATED
American Cancer Society, Philadelphia   (215) 665-2900
Cancer Information Service   1(800) 4-CANCER
Foundation for Adv. in Cancer Therapy   (610) 642-4810

CEREBRAL PALSY
Cerebral Palsy Assoc., Phila., PA   (215) 242-4200

CROHN'S & COLITIS RELATED
Crohn's & Colitis Foundation   (610) 354-8525
Feasterville, PA
A network of groups that meet at area hospitals.

DIABETES
American Diabetes Association   (610) 828-5003
Juvenile Diabetes Foundation   (215) 567-4307

DISEASE OR INJURY RELATED

HEART RELATED
American Heart Association (610) 940-9540
The Zipper Club (cardiac surgery) (215) 887-6644
Strive (info. for young stroke victims) (610) 828-6876

HEMOPHILIA (215) 885-6500
Hemophilia Foundation of Delaware Valley
Philadelphia, PA

HYSTERECTOMY RELATED
H.E.R.S. Foundation (610) 667-7757
 (215) 387-6700
Blackwell Birth Center for Women (215) 923-7577
Information/support for women dealing with hysterectomy.

KIDNEY DISEASE
American Kidney Foundation of Del. Valley (215) 923-8611
Philadelphia, PA
Support groups for adults and children undergoing kidney operations, as well as their families and friends.

LEUKEMIA (215) 232-1100
Leukemia Society of America
Monthly family support group meetings.

LIVER DISEASE
American Liver Foundation 1(800) 223-0179
Support groups for adults and children undergoing liver operations, as well as their families and friends.

LUNG DISEASE (215) 546-5820
American Lung Association (610) 239-9766
Philadelphia, PA
Support groups for asthma sufferers, ex-smokers and lung patients.

LUPUS (215) 743-7171
Lupus Foundation of Philadelphia
Support groups for patients with systematic lupus erythematosus.

MENTAL ILLNESS
Alliance for the Mentally Ill of Eastern PA (215) 572-1394
Philadelphia, PA
Offers monthly meetings for families of the mentally ill.

NERVOUS/EMOTIONAL ILLNESS
Recovery, Inc. (215) 332-0722
Offers self-help support groups for persons suffering from nervous or emotional illness.

PARKINSON DISEASE
American Parkinson Disease Assoc. (215) 342-6689
Philadelphia, PA
Monthly meetings, self-help groups and a hotline for family members.

LOCAL SUPPORTIVE ORGANIZATIONS
Page 89

SEXUALLY TRANSMITTED DISEASES
Philadelphia Help Group (herpes)   (215) 763-2247
C.D.C. National STD   1(800) 227-8922 (Hotline)

OTHER SUPPORT GROUPS

CONTACT PHILADELPHIA, INC.   (215) 877-9099

Free. They do telephone reassurance and call (at prearranged times) to check on and converse with elderly/homebound persons (or start emergency procedures if there is no reply).

COUNSELING AND SUPPORT GROUPS
Family Service of Bucks County	(215) 757-6916
Family Service of Chester County	(610) 696-4900
Family & Social Service of Delaware County	(610) 566-7540
Family Service of Montgomery County	(610) 272-1520
Family Service of Philadelphia County	(215) 875-3300
Youth & Family Services, NJ State Hotline	1(800) 331-DYFS (Hotline)
Youth & Family Services, NJ Southern Reg.	(609) 567-0010
Catholic Social Services, Philadelphia	(215) 587-3900
Catholic Family Life Bureau, South Jersey	(609) 756-7957
Episcopal Community Services, Phila. area	(215) 351-1400
Jewish Family & Children's Service, Phila. area	(215) 545-3290
Jewish Family & Children's Service, S. NJ	(609) 662-8611
Lutheran Children & Fam. Serv. of E. PA	(215) 276-7800
Samaritan Counseling Center, PA	(215) 247-6077

Many of these organizations have offices in several locations. Most offer all types of support groups, individual counseling and lend their facilities to a variety of support organizations for meetings. The religious organizations offer many things that the County Services do, but they also have groups that have religion in common. Usually, their counselors have been trained in psychology. Samaritan Counseling Center is in 8 areas, is inter-religious and doesn't discuss religion unless you do.

HOSPITALS IN THE DELAWARE VALLEY

Most offer free support groups; if they don't have what you need, ask if they know of another hospital that does. To give you an example, Montgomery Hospital offers support groups for: Alcoholics Anonymous, Bereavement, Insulin Pump users, Laryngectomy, Prostate Cancer, Diabetes, Breast Cancer, Cancer and Huntingdon's Disease.

LONG DISTANCE LOVE ("LDL")
P.O. Box 114
New Brunswick, NJ 08903

A non-profit network that pairs adults and children with peers who are suffering from similar handicaps, injuries or illnesses. Participants communicate by mail, cassette, telephone and videotape. Describe what you are looking for, and send a stamped self-addressed envelope to the above address. A $10 fee is requested.

Page 90 DIVORCED / SEPARATED / IN MOURNING / WIDOWED

NATIONAL SELF-HELP CLEARING HOUSE (212) 354-8525
New York, NY

Will try to match you with the support group you need, locally or nationally. Possibilities include groups seeking leads for rare disorders, self-help for endometriosis patients, support for the very short or tall and computer groups for the homebound. Based in Manhattan.

PARENT EXCHANGE (215) 242-9501

For families whose children are chronically ill or disabled. This is a way to share information about medical care, recreation, schools, transportation, funding and support groups.

PHILADELPHIA CANDLELIGHTERS (215) 884-0413

Support for families of catastrophically ill children.

DIVORCED / SEPARATED / IN MOURNING / WIDOWED

HOTLINES

Contact Philadelphia (215) 879-4402

For people who are distressed and in need of someone to talk to.

First Call For Help (United Way) (215) 568-3750

A referral information service of self-help groups in the area.

SUPPORT GROUPS

AMERICAN ASSOCIATION OF SUICIDOLOGY (303) 692-0985
2459 South Ash
Denver, CO 80222

This organization can provide national information about support groups for those who have lost a loved one through suicide.

CHURCH AND TEMPLE SUPPORT GROUPS

If you belong to the congregation of a church or temple, the obvious thing for you to do is ask what support groups they may offer. It is common to see support groups listed in the newspaper that meet at a church or temple. Don't assume that religion is an integral part of the group; many places allow their facilities to be used by independent support organizations. Ask ahead of time if it matters to you.

COMPASSIONATE FRIENDS, INC. (215) 884-6691
Philadelphia Chapter

A national organization of groups for bereaved siblings, grandparents and parents. Support is offered for loss at any point, from a miscarriage to the loss of an adult child. **Ask about groups in other areas.** The main organization is based in Oakbrook, Illinois (708) 990-0010.

LOCAL SUPPORTIVE ORGANIZATIONS   Page 91

COUNSELING AND SUPPORT GROUPS
Family Service of Bucks County	(215) 757-6916
Family Service of Chester County	(610) 696-4900
Family & Social Service of Delaware County	(610) 566-7540
Family Service of Montgomery County	(610) 272-1520
Family Service of Philadelphia County	(215) 875-3300
Youth & Family Services, NJ State Hotline	1(800) 331-DYFS (Hotline)
Youth & Family Services, NJ Southern Reg.	(609) 567-0010
Catholic Social Services, Philadelphia	(215) 587-3900
Catholic Family Life Bureau, South Jersey	(609) 756-7957
Episcopal Community Services, Phila. area	(215) 351-1400
Jewish Family & Children's Service, Phila. area	(215) 545-3290
Jewish Family & Children's Service, S. NJ	(609) 662-8611
Lutheran Children & Fam. Serv. of E. PA	(215) 276-7800
Samaritan Counseling Center, PA	(215) 247-6077

Many of these organizations have offices in several locations. Most offer all types of support groups, individual counseling and lend their facilities to a variety of support organizations for meetings. The religious organizations offer many things that the County Services do, but they also have groups that have religion in common. Usually, their counselors have been trained in psychology. Samaritan Counseling Center is in 8 areas, is inter-religious and doesn't discuss religion unless you do.

COUNSELING NETWORK   (215) 624-8190
FOR LOSS & TRANSITION

A widow and widower counseling and referral service.

FAMILIES OF MURDER VICTIMS, INC.   (215) 686-8078

FRESH-START DIVORCE SUPPORT GROUPS   (610) 644-6464
Fresh Start Seminars
Paoli, PA

This organization gives seminars that teach churches and other organizations how to run Fresh-Start divorce support groups. Therefore, they can help you locate a group in your area.

HELPING OTHER PEOPLE EVOLVE   (609) 461-1012
South New Jersey   (609) 654-6404

H.O.P.E. is for the recently widowed. There are 8 chapters thus far.

HOMICIDE SUPPORT GROUPS
Victim Services Center (Montgomery Cnty.)   (610) 272-3050 (Hotline)

For Montgomery County residents. However, you can always try calling to see if they know of similar groups in other counties.

HOSPITAL SUPPORT GROUPS

Hospitals nearly always have one or several types of "Bereavement" support groups; usually run by the hospice department. The "Neighbors" section of the Sunday <u>Philadelphia Inquirer</u> and local newspapers will list self-help/support groups offered by hospitals.

Page 92 DIVORCED / SEPARATED / IN MOURNING / WIDOWED

MADD   (Mothers Against Drunk Drivers)   (215) 332-7177
Philadelphia, PA

"Mothers Against Drunk Drivers." A support organization for injured victims, relatives and friends of people killed by drunk drivers.

THE MEN'S RESOURCE CENTER   (610) 971-9310
Wayne, PA

Counterpart to the Women's Resource Center but run by a different organization. Offers individual counseling, group therapy, workshops & seminars, outdoor team building workshops and therapeutic trips.

NATIONAL ORGANIZATION FOR WOMEN
State Chapter Office   (215) 351-5334
Philadelphia, PA

Philadelphia Chapter Office   (215) 922-6040
Cherry Hill Chapter Office   (609) 393-0156

"NOW" is the largest civil rights organization for women in the country. Among many other things, they offer free support groups for widowed, separated or divorced women.

NEW BEGINNINGS   (609) 756-7900

Sponsored by the Catholic Church, Camden Diocese. Offers various discussion/support groups.

NEWSPAPER LISTINGS

For this category, it can be helpful to look through your newspaper for local listings. The Sunday Philadelphia Inquirer "Neighbors" section has a Bulletin Board where local meetings are listed, and most local papers have something similar. Listings will usually include support groups that meet at hospitals, churches, libraries, therapist offices and other nearby locations. More importantly, listings sometimes include less common support groups such as those specifically for pet bereavement.

PARENTS WITHOUT PARTNERS

For detailed info., look under the Singles and Social Groups category of *Special Interest Organizations* in this book.

SINGLE PARENTS   (215) 947-8200
Gloria Dei Church
Huntingdon Valley, PA

Free. Relaxed discussions held on a regular basis (free child care).

SINGLE PARENTS SOCIETY

For detailed info., look under the Singles and Social Groups category of *Special Interest Organizations* in this book.

SUDDEN INFANT DEATH SYNDROME FDN.   (215) 222-1400
National Office
Philadelphia, PA   (Center City)

Offers SIDS support groups. Call to ask about locations.

LOCAL SUPPORTIVE ORGANIZATIONS

SURVIVORS OF SUICIDE
Philadelphia/Montgomery County   (215) 545-2242
Delaware County   (610) 586-5171

Support group for relatives and friends of suicides.

THEOS   (412) 471-7779
"To Help Each Other Spiritually"
National Headquarters
Pittsburgh, PA

A national support group organization for widows and widowers. Contact the national Office and they will tell you who to contact locally. Groups generally meet twice a month on an ongoing basis, year-round.

TO LIVE AGAIN (TLA Central Office)   (610) 353-7740
P.O. Box 415
Springfield, PA 19064

Support groups for widowed people (monthly meetings, peer support and outings). Call for a group in your area.

UNITE, INC.   (215) 728-3777

Grief support groups for those who have lost a baby or had a miscarriage.

WIDOW & WIDOWER   (215) 947-8654
Huntingdon Valley, PA

Weekly support groups for those who have lost a mate through death. Followed by refreshments and a social hour. Small fee.

WIDOW & WIDOWER   (610) 896-7770
Kaiserman Jewish Community Center
Wynnewood, PA

A support group that meets twice a month. Small attendance fee.

WOMEN IN TRANSITION   (215) 922-9500 (Hotline)
Philadelphia, PA (Center City)   (215) 564-5301

Offers various support groups and workshops. Fees vary from free to sliding scale.

THE WOMEN'S RESOURCE CENTER   (610) 687-6391
113 West Wayne Avenue   Mon.–Thurs. 9:30–3:00
P.O. Box 309
Wayne, PA 19087

By phone they give referrals and suggestions. On site they offer workshops; free drop-in counseling; legal consultations; and support groups for single mothers (no charge), divorce, career and divorce financial issues. A mid-life group meets for brunch; a social group meets for dinners, etc. Sliding scale rates may be available. Memb. is $25/yr.

YOUNG WIDOW & WIDOWER
Media, PA   (610) 896-5720
Elkins Park, PA   (215) 663-6000

Bi-monthly support groups for people under age 45, (or over 45 but with a child or teenager at home). Usually followed by a social hour. Optional small door fee.

FAMILY GROUP / FAMILY INDIVIDUALS / CHILDREN

HOTLINES

Contact Philadelphia (215) 877-9099
For people who are distressed and in need of someone to talk to.

Daemion House Adolescents' Crisis Hot Line (610) 647-1431

Fathers' Rights (610) 688-4748
Fathers' and Children's hotline with referral information.

First Call For Help (United Way) (215) 568-3750
A referral information service for self-help groups in the area.

Suicide & Crisis Intervention Service (215) 686-4420

Warmline 1(800) 628-2535
Sponsored by Parents Network. For parents wishing to speak to a trained facilitator about concerns they have with child development.

Youth Crisis Line 1(800) 448-4663

SUPPORT GROUPS

HELPFUL HINT: Remember, if the fees are too high, it doesn't hurt to ask if reduced rates or scholarships are available (some organizations do offer them). If you want to find an organization that offers low cost family therapy (together or individually) try contacting your child's school guidance counselor. Otherwise, call your local Family Community Services office and ask them what support groups they offer, and if they know of other sliding-scale fee counseling organizations in the area. (Every community has at least one official one and a few semi-official ones.)

ADOPTION FORUM (215) 238-1116
Philadelphia, PA

Offers support groups for adoptees, birth parents and adoptive parents. They can tell you about meetings all over the Delaware Valley. Most groups meet once a month, some meet twice. The (Center City) Philadelphia group meets on the 3rd Sunday, monthly.

BIG BROTHER-BIG SISTER
National Headquarters (215) 567-7000
Philadelphia, PA

Philadelphia Branch (215) 557-8600
Philadelphia, PA

Volunteers become a substitute brother-sister to children or teenagers who are from distressed families. These are not necessarily children who live in slums or in poverty; they may simply be kids who've lost a parent through divorce or death.

LOCAL SUPPORTIVE ORGANIZATIONS

THE BIRTH CENTER   (610) 525-6086
Bryn Mawr, PA

Support groups for new mothers with babies up to 1 year old. Infant massage classes, and programs for parents with children 1-3 years old.

BIRTH ORIENTED RESOURCE NETWORK   (215) 675-5506
Horsham, PA

A support group for people with birthing and parenting issues. They advocate home-birth, breast feeding, cloth diapers, non-circumcision, and informed immunization.

CAREGIVER SUPPORT GROUPS

These are meant to address the emotional needs of people who care for elderly or very ill people. To locate groups near you, buy the Sunday Philadelphia Inquirer and look at the Neighbors section. Your local newspapers may have something similar. Under the category of "Support Groups" you will probably notice one or more titled "Caregiver"; these are often sponsored by hospitals or churches.

CATHOLIC FAMILY LIFE BUREAU   (609) 756-7957
South Jersey

Call to find out about local programs and services.

CATHOLIC SOCIAL SERVICES OF PHILA.   (215) 587-3900
Main Office
Philadelphia, PA

Call to find out about support programs in and outside of Philadelphia.

CENTER CITY HOME SCHOOLERS   (215) 732-7723
2203 Spruce Street   (215) 482-7933
Philadelphia, PA 19103

A Home Schooling support group and resource organization. Monthly meetings are the 1st Thursday at 10:00 am (kids welcomed).

CHILD AND PARENT CENTER   (215) 829-5555
Hall-Mercer Center
Pennsylvania Hospital
Philadelphia, PA

Support groups for single parents, working mothers, teens and adoptive parents. Workshops on various child/parent issues. Fees vary.

CHILDREN OF AGING PARENTS, INC. (CAPS)   (215) 945-6900

Maintains a national network of caregiver support groups which meet regularly. Provides referral and resource information. They have a small membership fee.

CHRISTIAN CHURCH GROUPS FOR ALL AGES
The Christian Support Guide   1(800) 798-7023
for Bucks and Montgomery Counties

A free magazine with 6 pages of Protestant church based support groups. Groups include: youth, senior citizens, Scouts, singles, women, choirs, softball, Bible study, and fellowships. Also has 3rd party support groups such as Narcotics Anonymous, To Live Again and A. A.

Page 96 — FAMILY GROUP / FAMILY INDIVIDUALS / CHILDREN

EPISCOPAL COMMUNITY SERVICES (215) 351-1400
Philadelphia, PA

They offer various programs and support services. Call to find out about local programs and services in and outside of Philadelphia.

FAMILY & SOCIAL SERVICE OF DELAWARE COUNTY
Clifton Heights, PA (610) 626-5800
Media, PA (610) 566-7540

Offers workshops and support groups of all kinds. Sliding scale fees.

FAMILY CONNECTIONS (610) 446-2990
United Methodist Church
Bala Cynwyd, PA

Playgroups (from birth on up), support groups (childcare available), workshops, annual events, and holiday parties. Fees vary with the activity.

FAMILY FORUM (610) 688-8888
Wayne, PA

Has support groups and courses and seminars in effective parenting skills. Sample topics include "How to handle adolescent sons and daughters" and "Sibling rivalry."

FAMILY LEARNING CENTER (215) 836-5060
Flourtown, PA

Step-parent discussion group meets 1st Wednesday monthly. Free, but pre-registration is required.

FAMILY SERVICE OF BUCKS COUNTY:
Bristol, PA (215) 781-3999
Doylestown, PA (215) 345-0550
Langhorne, PA (215) 757-6916
Quakertown, PA (215) 538-1616

Workshops and support groups of all kinds. Sliding scale fees.

FAMILY SERVICE OF CHESTER COUNTY:
Coatesville, PA (610) 384-1926
Kennett Square, PA (610) 444-5652
West Chester, PA (610) 696-4900

Workshops and support groups of all kinds. Sliding scale fees.

FAMILY SERVICE OF MONTGOMERY COUNTY:
Bryn Mawr, PA (610) 527-5354
Lansdale, PA (610) 368-0985
Norristown, PA (Main Office) (610) 272-1520
Pottstown, PA (610) 326-1610
Willow Grove, PA (610) 657-7141

Workshops and support groups of all kinds. Sliding scale fees.

FAMILY SERVICE OF PHILADELPHIA:
Main Office (215) 875-3300

Workshops and support groups of all kinds. Sliding scale fees.

LOCAL SUPPORTIVE ORGANIZATIONS   Page 97

FATHERS & CHILDREN EQUALITY   (610) 688-4748
Information support organization for father custody and visitation rights.

FATHERS & CHILDREN TOGETHER ("FACT")   (215) 727-0708
Support group for fathers with divorce custody issues. Promotes both parents for children. Meets weekly at Frankfort YWCA. Memb. $20/yr.

FIRST CALL FOR HELP (UNITED WAY)   (215) 568-3750
A telephone support and guidance service.

INCEST SURVIVORS ANONYMOUS   (215) 848-3830
Philadelphia, PA
12-step program. Support groups for survivors of child sexual abuse. They also offer women-only meetings.

JEWISH FAMILY & CHILDREN'S SERVICE
Central Philadelphia, PA	(215) 545-3290
Main Line, PA	(610) 896-8180
Northeast Philadelphia	(215) 673-0100
Northeast walk-in service	(215) 673-7741
Northwest Philadelphia	(215) 635-8909
South Jersey	(609) 662-8611

Workshops and support groups of all kinds. Sliding scale fees.

LA LECHE LEAGUE
National Office	1 (800) La-Leche
Local Contact Information Hotline	(610) 666-0359 (Hotline)
La Leche League of Central Philadelphia	(610) 647-7769
La Leche League of Northeast Philadelphia	(215) 342-0233

Breast-feeding support groups are held at various locations. They offer guidance in breast feeding and parenting skills.

LEARNING DISABILITIES ASSOC. OF PA   (610) 458-8193
This is the State Office. They can refer you to local support groups.

LUTHERAN CHILDREN & FAMILY SERVICE   (215) 276-7800
OF E. PENNSYLVANIA
Philadelphia, PA
Offers various programs and support services. Call to find out about local programs and services in and outside of Philadelphia.

MOMS CLUB
The National Headquarters Office in CA	(805) 526-2725
The Regional Representative for DE	(410) 750-9427
The Regional Representative for PA and NJ	(610) 873-8995

Contact the regional representative for information on any groups near you. The King of Prussia group (below) is an example of one local group.

MOMS CLUB
King of Prussia/Wayne, PA
Monthly activity group based around the King of Prussia/Wayne area (but any mom can join the group). Children are welcome at meetings. Memb. $15/yr. Call PA representative (see above) for current contacts.

Page 98 FAMILY GROUP / FAMILY INDIVIDUALS / CHILDREN

MOTHERS' ASSOCIATIONS

Initially meant for breastfeeding mothers, these groups sometimes also have members with formula-fed children. They generally provide a supportive network for parenting issues and meet once or twice a month for a combination children's playgroup/mother get-together. New mothers can receive the free telephone support of an assigned "Counselor" if they want to. **There are many groups in the Delaware Valley. To locate the Nursing Mothers Group near you call the hotline shown below**:

NURSING MOTHERS' ADVISORY COUNCIL (215) 572-8044 (Hotline)

Will refer you to one of many workshop/support groups in the area. The ones I know of are in: Abington, Ambler, Germantown-Roxborough, Harleysville, Hatfield, Huntingdon Valley, King of Prussia, Mt. Airy-Chestnut Hill, Norristown, North Wales, Malvern-Exton, Merion-Wynnefield, Springfield-Broomall-Drexel Hill, Lansdowne, Wayne-Paoli and West Chester. But I am certain that there are more.

MOTHERS OF TWINS CLUB (505) 275-0955
National Organization
P.O. Box 23188
Albuquerque, NM 87192-1188

A support organization for families with twins. They have regular gatherings and sponsor activities (like clothes/equipment swap meetings).
There is no Center City group, but there are groups in many other areas. The Valley Forge club meets in King of Prussia, and I know there is also a group in South Jersey.

MOTHERS WITHOUT CUSTODY 1(800) 457-6962
National Support Group
P.O. Box 27418
Houston, Texas 77227-7418

Call for support and to see if there are any support groups in your area.

NATIONAL SELF-HELP CLEARING HOUSE (212) 354-8525
New York, NY

Will match you with the support group that you need, locally or nationally. Possibilities include groups seeking leads for rare disorders, self-help for anorexics or endometriosis patients, support for the very short or tall, and computer groups for the homebound. Based in Manhattan.

NEIGHBORHOOD PARENTING PROGRAMS (PHILADELPHIA)
Community Women's Education Project (215) 425-7990
Frankford Ave. and Somerset St.
or,
Neighborhood Parenting Program (215) 535-8840

PARENT ACTION NETWORK OF PHILA. (215) 686-8650
Philadelphia, PA

Offers weekly support groups for parents and programs in parenting at various hospitals, churches and hospitals.

LOCAL SUPPORTIVE ORGANIZATIONS

THE PARENT CENTER   (610) 527-5490
Phoebe Anna Thorne School
Bryn Mawr College
Bryn Mawr, PA

Offers once-a-week parent/infant drop-ins. Parents talk with each other, discuss child rearing and play with their children in a group (for children from newborn to age 3). They also offer discussion programs.

PARENT EDUCATION NETWORK ("PEN")   (717) 845-9722
333 East 7th Avenue   1(800) 522-5827
York, PA 17404

A network for parents of children with special needs, requiring special education. They maintain their 800 number for "Referral and consultation in identifying services or assistance within the parents' local area."

PARENT EXCHANGE   (215) 242-9501

For families of chronically ill or disabled children. A way to share information about medical care, recreation, schools, transportation, funding and support groups.

PARENT RESOURCE ASSOCIATION CENTER   (215) 576-7961
Wyncote, PA

Workshops and parent groups for parents of infants and toddlers.

PARENTS INC.   1(800) 628-25352 (Warmline)

The "Warmline" service answers parenting questions and questions about program locations. They have support groups and offer drop-in play and discussion groups. At least one branch offers workshops in infant CPR, effective discipline, toilet training, limit setting and more.

Fort Washington, PA (Parents Network)   (215) 628-2402
Philadelphia/Center City, PA   (215) 241-1700
Philadelphia/Northwest, PA (Chestnut Hill Hospital)
Philadelphia/North, PA (Jacob's Ladder Project)
Philadelphia Housing Authority Sites in PA (6 locations)
Lansdale, PA
Doylestown, PA
Southhampton, PA

PARENTS IN PROGRESS   (215) 755-2666
Philadelphia, PA

Offers playgroups, support and discussion groups.

PARENTS PROJECT   (609) 482-9522
Ramblewood Center
Mount Laurel, NJ

Has classes and workshops in parenting skills. They also offer events for single parents, parents of disabled children and step-families. Fees vary.

PARENTS SUPPORTING PARENTS   (610) 272-3050
Norristown, Conshohocken, PA

Support group meetings for parents feeling unsure about their skills or simply feeling overwhelmed. Childcare provided during meetings.

Page 100 FAMILY GROUP / FAMILY INDIVIDUALS / CHILDREN

PARENTS WITHOUT PARTNERS
For detailed information on all branches see <u>Singles and Social Groups</u> under *Special Interest Organizations*.

POSITIVE PARENTING (215) 362-5244
Lansdale, PA

Resource center with playgroups and workshops (includes a series on sibling-rivalry).

PRACTICAL PARENTING (610) 696-5025
West Chester, PA

Has workshops such as "Surviving, thriving with difficult children," programs and support groups.

RESOLVE, Inc. (215) 849-3920
They provide information about infertility and will tell you about support groups in your area.

SAMARITAN COUNSELING CENTER
Abington, PA	(215) 659-1216
Ambler, PA	(215) 643-5826
Hatboro, PA	(215) 675-8646
Chestnut Hill, PA	(215) 247-6077
Doylestown, PA	(215) 345-5929
Feasterville, PA	(215) 357-7777
Germantown, PA	(215) 438-5696
Morrisville, PA	(215) 295-4585

This is an umbrella organization of churches (Baptist, Presbyterian and Lutheran) that offer interfaith social services, counseling, psychotherapy, workshops and more. Religion is not a part of the counseling unless you desire it. Sliding scale fees.

SINGLE PARENT ACTIVITIES AND PROGRAMS
Jewish Community Center, Kaiserman Branch (610) 896-7770
Wynnewood, PA
and
Jewish Community Center, Klein Branch (215) 698-7300
Philadelphia, PA
and
Jewish Community Center, of S. New Jersey (609) 662-8800
Cherry Hill, NJ

Seminars and social activities for single parents.

SINGLE PARENTS SOCIETY (215) 928-9443
Call them for info. on all branches. Also, see <u>Singles and Social Groups</u> under *Special Interest Organizations* for more detailed information.

TOUGHLOVE INTERNATIONAL (215) 348-7090
1(800) 333-1069

For parents with out-of-control children. Call to find out about group meetings in various locations.

LOCAL SUPPORTIVE ORGANIZATIONS Page 101

WELL SPOUSE FOUNDATION   (212) 724-7209
National Headquarters   1(800) 838-0879
P.O. Box 801
New York, NY 10023

A support organization for mates of disabled or chronically ill spouses. They will tell you about support groups in your area. The local Philadelphia support group is in Elkins Park; call (215) 673-9487.

YOUTH & FAMILY SERVICES, NJ STATE   1(800) 331-DYFS (Hotline)
YOUTH & FAMILY SERVICES, NJ S. REGION (609) 567-0010

Call the Hotline number for information about local Youth & Family offices and the support groups/counseling/services they offer. If that doesn't work, try the second (regional) number.

HANDICAPPED / DISABLED PERSONS

HOTLINES

Mayor's Office for the Handicapped   (215) 686-2798

SERVICES

EDUCATIONAL INFORMATION AND   (609) 582-7000
RESOURCE CENTER
700 Hollydell Court
Sewell, NJ 08080

A "Learning Resource Center" for parents and teachers of handicapped children. You can borrow books, toys, games or videos. Memb. $2.

LIBRARY FOR THE BLIND   (215) 925-3213
AND PHYSICALLY DISABLED
Free Library of Philadelphia
919 Walnut Street
Philadelphia, PA 19107

Join the library and you'll have access to talking books, cassettes, large print books and braille books.

MAGEE REHABILITATION HOSPITAL   (215) 587-3000
6 Franklin Plaza
Philadelphia, PA 19102

Offers a large number of support groups and a major wheelchair sports event program. They also act as an information/resource center for the disabled.

MOSS REHABILITATION HOSPITAL   (215) 456-9900
1200 West Tabor Road
Philadelphia, PA 19141   (North Philadelphia

Offers a large number of support groups; also acts as an information and resource center for the disabled.

HANDICAPPED / DISABLED PERSONS

PA DEPARTMENT ON AGING (717) 783-1550
231 State Street, Barto Bldg.
Harrisburg, PA 17101-1195

Despite its title, this department also oversees services to the physically handicapped (age 18+) through area agencies. The agencies, in turn, provide information and referral services for programs and activities available to disabled and handicapped persons.

Bucks County (Doylestown, PA)	(215) 348-0510
Chester County (West Chester), PA	(610) 344-6350
Delaware County (Media), PA	(610) 891-4455
Philadelphia Corporation for the Aging, PA	(215) 765-9000
Montgomery County (Norristown, PA)	(610) 278-3601

SPORTS

See the description of **Moss Rehabilitation Hospital** and **Magee Rehabilitation Hospital**, they both have athletic programs.

Also see the Sports section of *Special Interest Organizations*.

SUPPORT GROUPS

ACTION ALLIANCE FOR PARENTS (215) 951-0300
OF THE DEAF (610) 825-4568

ASSOCIATED SERVICES FOR THE BLIND (215) 627-0600

Group counseling and support groups for visually impaired persons and their families.

LONG DISTANCE LOVE ("LDL")
P.O. Box 114
New Brunswick, NJ 08903

A non-profit network that pairs adults and children with peers suffering from similar handicaps/injuries/illnesses. They communicate by mail/cassette/telephone and videotape. Send stamped, self-addressed envelope and describe what you are looking for. A $10 fee is requested.

NATIONAL CENTER FOR STUTTERING 1(800) 221-2483 (Hotline)

NATIONAL DOWN SYNDROME CONGRESS 1(800) 232-NDSC

Contact them for support groups in your area.

NATIONAL DOWN SYNDROME SOCIETY 1(800) 221-4602

Contact them for support groups in your area.

NATIONAL SELF-HELP CLEARING HOUSE (212) 354-8525
New York, NY

Will match you with the support group that you need, locally or nationally. Possibilities include groups seeking leads for rare disorders, self-help for anorexics or endometriosis patients, support for the very short or tall, and computer groups for the homebound. Based in Manhattan.

LOCAL SUPPORTIVE ORGANIZATIONS

NATIONAL STUTTERING PROJECT   (215) 664-5139
Philadelphia Chapter

Meetings feature group discussions, guest speakers, and opportunities to improve fluency.

THE ORTON DYSLEXIA SOCIETY   (610) 527-1548
Box 251
Bryn Mawr, PA 19010

Offers seminars, parent support groups and more.

PARENT EXCHANGE   (215) 229-4550

Families of chronically ill or disabled children share info. about medical care, recreation, schools, transportation, funding and support groups.

PARENTS NETWORK   (215) 229-4550

PARENTS SUPPORTING PARENTS   (610) 272-3050
1354 Valley Road
Villanova, PA 19085

Parents of children with attention deficit disorder. Offers support groups, telephone support groups, professional referrals.

Also see other categories under *Local Supportive Organizations*.

TRAVEL INFORMATION

"ACCESS TO THE WORLD: A TRAVEL GUIDE FOR THE HANDICAPPED"
By Louise Weiss. Henry Holt & Co. Publishers.

AMTRAK CUSTOMER RELATIONS
400 North Capital St.
N.W. Washington, DC 20001

Publishes "Access Amtrak," a free guide to their services for the elderly and disabled.

TRAVEL INFORMATION CENTER   (215) 329-5715
Moss Rehabilitation Hospital
12th St. and Tabor Rd.
Philadelphia, PA 19141

Supplies information for up to 3 destinations (sights, accommodations and transportation) for small fee. Also supplies names of travel agencies which specialize in travel plans for the disabled.

LEGAL OR FINANCIAL ADVICE

COMMUNITY LEGAL SERVICES
Philadelphia, PA　　　　　　　　　(215) 893-5300
N. Central　　　　　　　　　　　　(215) 227-2400
Northeast　　　　　　　　　　　　(215) 427-4850
South　　　　　　　　　　　　　　(215) 271-2500
West　　　　　　　　　　　　　　 (215) 471-2200

Provides free individual and educational legal assistance to low income persons and those in financial distress. For Philadelphia residents (civil action only).

LEGAL SERVICES FOR OTHER COUNTIES:
Bucks County Legal Aid　　　　　　(215) 781-1111
Legal Aid of Chester County　　　　(610) 436-9150
Delaware County Legal Aid　　　　 (610) 490-6900
Montgomery County Legal Aid　　　(610) 275-5400

All of these provide free civil legal aid to those in distressed finances.

LAWYER REFERRAL SERVICES
Philadelphia　　　　　　　　　　　(215) 238-1701
Chester County　　　　　　　　　 (610)436-9150
Delaware County　　　　　　　　 (610) 874-8421
Montgomery County　　　　　　　(610) 279-9660, #5

Depending on the type of legal problem you have, these organizations can often refer you to a lawyer who might offer reduced rates.

LEGAL HOTLINE FOR OLDER AMERICANS　　1(800) 262-5297

For questions that can be answered over the telephone. In general, those who are 60 or older with social or economic needs are eligible.

PA LAWYER REFERRAL SERVICE　　1(800) 692-7375

Issues listings of lawyers in each county.

PHILADELPHIA BAR ASSOC. LEGAL LINE:　　(215) 238-1701

A phone line for free legal counseling. Open the 1st and 3rd Wednesdays of each month from 5:30 pm to 8 pm.

PHILADELPHIA VOLUNTEER LAWYERS　　(215) 545-3385
FOR THE ARTS

For artists of all types and for art groups. Free legal referrals, a research library, seminars, publications, etc.

PUBLIC INTEREST LAW CENTER OF PHILA.　　(215) 627-7100

Free civil legal aid, counseling, analysis, negotiation and litigation.

TEMPLE ELDERLY LAW PROJECT　　(215) 204-7869
Temple University School Of Law
Legal Aid Office

Low cost civil legal aid for people who are financially distressed.

WOMEN AGAINST ABUSE LEGAL CENTER (215) 686-7082
Philadelphia, PA

Free legal counseling and court representation for abuse cases.

WOMEN'S LAW PROJECT (215) 928-9801
125 S. 9th Street
Philadelphia, PA

A non-profit organization of volunteers who give free legal advice by telephone. The person who initially speaks to you will remain your counselor for subsequent conversations. Call early because you will have to leave a message asking them to call. They always do call back but, if you call too late, it may not be until the next day.

Also see the "Divorced/Separated/In Mourning/Widowed", "Men's and Women's Issues" and "People Seeking Employment" categories of Local Supportive Organizations.

PROSPECTIVE SMALL BUSINESS OWNERS

HELPFUL HINTS: Free for people who want to start a small business. They offer services and management assistance in business plans, accounting/record keeping, financial analysis, marketing plans and more. One to one counseling is usually available.

DREXEL UNIVERSITY (215) 895-2122
Dept. of Management
College of Business
Academic Building, Room 314
Philadelphia, PA   19104

LA SALLE UNIVERSITY (215) 951-1416/
Small Business Development Center (215) 951-1735
20th Street & Olney Avenue
Philadelphia, PA   19141

Facilities are accessible to the handicapped.

TEMPLE UNIVERSITY (215) 204-7282
Room 6, Speakman Hall—006-00
Small Business Development Center
Philadelphia, PA   19122

UNIVERSITY OF PENNSYLVANIA (215) 898-4861
Small Business Development Center
Wharton Business School
409 Vance Hall
Philadelphia, PA   19104-6357

VILLANOVA UNIVERSITY (610) 519-4382
Small Business Institute
Ithan and Lancaster Avenues
Villanova, PA   19085

This organization helps small, established businesses to solve problems. Also helps them to strengthen loan application materials.

WEST CHESTER UNIVERSITY　　　　　　(610) 363-5175
Small Business Development Center
930 East Lancaster Ave., Suite 201
Exton, PA 19341

OTHER OPTIONS AVAILABLE TO YOU:

BUREAU OF SMALL BUSINESS　　　　　(717) 783-5700
AND APPALACHIAN DEVELOPMENT
461 Forum Building
Harrisburg, PA 17120

"Interested in starting a business? Having a problem with a state agency? Have a business question?" This agency is Pennsylvania's "Single point contact" for small business. They answer state related and general business questions about licenses and permits.

BUREAU OF WOMEN'S BUSINESS DEVEL.　(717) 787-3339
Office of Small Business
462 Forum Building
Harrisburg, PA 17120

"Provides information and technical assistance to women in all phases of business development. Referral services may include entrepreneurial, management, and financial skills training, contracting opportunities, business counseling, and networking."

COMMUNITY ACCOUNTANTS　　　　　(215) 662-0211
3508 Market Street (University City)
Philadelphia, PA

Helps small businesses with their accounting, for free. Many of the applicants are non-profit organizations; some are involved in the arts.

SMALL BUSINESS ADMINISTRATION　　(610) 962-3805
District Office
475 Allendale Road, Suite 201
King of Prussia, PA 19406

LOCAL SUPPORTIVE ORGANIZATIONS   Page 107

MEN'S AND WOMEN'S ISSUES

HOTLINES

AIDS Hotline (Philadelphia)	1(800) 662-6080
AIDS Hotline (National)	1(800) 342-2437

Contact Philadelphia   (215) 879-4402
Counseling & Crisis Hotline
For people who are distressed and in need of someone to talk to.

First Call for Help (United Way)   (215) 568-3750
A referral information service of self-help groups in the area.

Mayor's Commission for Women   (215) 686-2171
Philadelphia, PA

National Alliance for the Mentally Ill   1(800) 950-NAMI

PLGTF Hotline   (215) 722-2005
To report anti-Lesbian and anti-Gay violence and discrimination.

Pregnancy Advice / Contraceptive Advice:
    Planned Parenthood   (215) 351-5560
                                          (215) 923-5211
    Blackwell Health Center for Women   (215) 923-7577

Rape Crisis Center (South Jersey)   (609) 858-7800
                                          1(800) 491-WATCH (in NJ)
Delaware County Women Against Rape   (610) 566-4342
Rape Crisis Center (Montgomery County)   (610) 277-5200
Rape Crisis Council (Chester County)   (610) 692-RAPE
Rape Crisis (Delaware)   (302) 575-1112

Women Organized Against Rape   (215) 985-3333
Philadelphia, PA

Suicide & Crisis Intervention Services   (215) 686-4420
Philadelphia, PA

Women Against Abuse   (215) 386-7777

Women in Transition   (215) 751-1111

MEN AND WOMEN

HELPFUL HINTS: Listing every individual branch of the following organizations would take up hundreds of pages. You can call the number I've listed and ask if there is a branch or group near to you. Remember that groups that meet at religious buildings are often not religious in nature themselves. Another option is to buy the Sunday <u>Philadelphia Inquirer</u> and look at the community "Bulletin Board" page. It will list various support meetings in your area.

MEN'S AND WOMEN'S ISSUES

COUNSELING AND SUPPORT GROUPS

Family Service of Bucks County	(215) 757-6916
Family Service of Chester County	(610) 696-4900
Family & Social Service of Delaware County	(610) 566-7540
Family Service of Montgomery County	(610) 272-1520
Family Service of Philadelphia County	(215) 875-3300
Youth & Family Services, NJ State Hotline	1(800) 331-DYFS (Hotline)
Youth & Family Services, NJ Southern Reg.	(609) 567-0010
Catholic Social Services, Philadelphia	(215) 587-3900
Catholic Family Life Bureau, South Jersey	(609) 756-7957
Episcopal Community Services, Phila. area	(215) 351-1400
Jewish Family & Children's Service, Phila. area	(215) 545-3290
Jewish Family & Children's Service, S. NJ	(609) 662-8611
Lutheran Children & Fam. Serv. of E. PA	(215) 276-7800
Samaritan Counseling Center, PA	(215) 247-6077

Many of these have offices in several locations. Most offer support groups, individual counseling and lend their facilities to other support organizations for meetings. The religious group counselors have usually been trained in psychology. Samaritan Counseling Center is in 8 areas, is inter-religious and doesn't discuss religion unless you do.

CRIME VICTIM CENTER (610) 692-7420

FLYING SOLO (215) 968-3861
Newtown, PA

Weekly support group for widowed, divorced, single or separated people.

GAY & LESBIAN SWITCHBOARD (215) 546-7100

INTERFAITH WORKING GROUP (215) 389-1400

Will provide a listing of gay-friendly congregations in the Philly area.

JEWISH FAMILY SERVICES (NJ) (609) 927-7475
Main Office in Linwood, NJ

A satellite office in Ventnor. Offers family and individual counseling.

N.A.A.F.A (215) 879-8588 (Tape)
National Association to Advance Fat Acceptance
Horsham, PA

Offers social events, newsletter and support groups. Memb. $10/yr.

NATIONAL SELF-HELP CLEARING HOUSE (212) 354-8525
New York, NY

Will match you with the support group that you need, locally or nationally. Possibilities include groups seeking leads for rare disorders, support for the very short or tall, and computer groups for the homebound.

NETWORK OF VICTIM ASSISTANCE 1(800) 675-6900

Provides services to victims of sexual assault. 9 am to 4:30 pm.

PARENTS, FAMILIES & FRIENDS (215) 572-1833 (Helpline)
OF LESBIANS AND GAYS

This support group helps members accept the lives of their loved ones.

LOCAL SUPPORTIVE ORGANIZATIONS

PENGUIN PLACE   (215) 732-2220 (Tape message)
Gay and Lesbian Community Center   (215) 732-8255 (Couns. Serv.)
201 South Camac Street
Philadelphia, PA 19107

Offers support groups, social gatherings, lectures and discussions.

PHILADELPHIA LESBIAN & GAY TASK FORCE   (215) 772-2000

RAPE AND CRIME VICTIM ASSISTANCE   (215) 842-4010
Medical College of Pennsylvania

Free evaluations, counseling and treatment for victims of rape, robbery, simple and aggravated assault.

RESOLVE, Inc.   (215) 849-3920
Philadelphia, PA

Organizes local support groups for couples dealing with infertility.

FOR MEN

MANTALK   (215) 844-8122
Philadelphia, PA (Mt. Airy)

Counseling and resource center with regular support-group meetings to address divorce, career, grief and loss, relationships, and parenthood.

THE MEN'S RESOURCE CENTER   (610) 971-9310
Wayne, PA

Individual counseling, group therapy, workshops & seminars, outdoor team-building workshops, and therapeutic trips.

Also see groups for men under the Family Group/Individuals/children category.

FOR WOMEN

N.O.W.
National Organization for Women
Philadelphia, PA (Center City)   (215) 351-5334
Cherry Hill, NJ   (609) 393-0156

Has various support groups for women, often for free.

SUPPORTIVE OLDER WOMEN'S NETWORK   (215) 477-6000

There are 45 support groups in the area. Members can use their "Telephone Reassurance" network program for crisis calls and birthdays.

WOMEN AGAINST ABUSE   (215) 386-1280
Philadelphia, PA   (215) 386-7777 (Hotline)

Offers crisis counseling, legal assistance, shelter, etc.

WOMEN IN TRANSITION   (215) 922-7500 (Hotline)
Philadelphia, PA (Center City)   (215) 564-5301

Workshops and support groups for mid-life transition, singlehood and parenting. Counseling for families and battered women, women involved with a drug or alcohol abuser, etc. Fees vary from free to sliding scale.

WOMEN ORGANIZED AGAINST RAPE   (215) 985-3315
                                      1(800) 985-3333 (Hotline)
Support groups and other supportive services.

WOMEN'S CENTER OF MONTGOMERY COUNTY
Jenkintown, PA   (610) 885-5020 (Hotline)
Norristown, PA   (610) 279-1548
Pottstown, PA   (610) 970-7363

Information and referrals, support for battered women (and protective service), job readiness training, job search support groups, legal counseling, self-help groups of various types. Some services are free and some have a fee.

THE WOMEN'S RESOURCE CENTER   (610) 687-6391
113 West Wayne Avenue   Mon.–Thurs. 9:30–3:00
P.O. Box 309
Wayne, PA   19087

A non-profit organization. Over the phone they'll give referrals, suggestions and contacts to non-members and members. On site they offer workshops; free drop-in counseling; free legal consultations; and support groups for divorce, career, divorce finanical issues, and for single mothers (free). There is a reference library. They also have a mid-life group that meets for brunch, a social group that meets for dinners and much more. Sliding scale rates may be available. Memb. $25/yr. (includes a monthly newsletter and discounts for activities.)

NEW RESIDENTS

HELPFUL HINTS: These are a few organizations that can help you feel at home more quickly. But as far as socializing goes, all you need to do is look though the book and focus on the categories that match your needs or interests. Have Fun!!

HOTLINES

Travelers Aid Society   (215) 546-0571
For newcomers as well as travelers.

The Talking Yellow Pages   (610) 337-7777
Dial the above number and then type code number for:

Local Weather Forecast #2400
Jersey Shore Forecast #2441
Poconos Forecast #2442
(Look in the Donnelley Directory Yellow pages for more options)

Special Events Recording #2116
Events for this Month #2553
(Look in the Donnelley Directory Yellow Pages for other selections ranging from Stock Market Reports and Sports Scores to Lottery Results.)

LOCAL SUPPORTIVE ORGANIZATIONS

INTRODUCTORY ORGANIZATIONS

WELCOME WAGON INTERNATIONAL   (215) 674-5105
Central number for the Delaware Valley area

If the Welcome Wagon people have not found you, call this number and they'll have a local representative get in touch. They might know about local newcomers groups.

"SHALOM" PROGRAM   (610) 356-9515
Jewish Information & Referral Services
Jewish Federation of Delaware County

This organization will send newcomers a packet of information about Jewish programs and services in the area.

NEWCOMERS GROUPS

"These are located in many communities. Typically, new members must have lived in the area for less than 2 or 3 years. However, as long as you join in that period, you can remain a member as long as you like. Members generally have monthly meetings and form special interest groups to do other activities. It's a way for new arrivals to get to know each other. The groups are entirely made up of volunteers, and the leaders change yearly. Some groups will contact you shortly after your arrival in a new area. However, it is often difficult to locate them if they don't find you. To locate a newcomers group in your area scan local newspapers and check bulletin boards at grocery stores or libraries. You can also ask neighbors, the Welcome Wagon representative, real estate sales people or the Chamber of Commerce. It's unfortunate that it's not easier, but it will be well worth your while to try and locate one."

                                      Lorna Espenshade (former member)
                                      Wayne, PA

These are the few groups that I have actually been able to track down. Most groups are *very* specific about their territory borders. I have also heard rumors of an "Upper Main Line Newcomers Group" (St.Davids-Radnor-Devon-Wayne), a group in Phoenixville, and a group in Doylestown. Since all of the groups are independent, they genuinely know absolutely *nothing* about each other and have *no* ability to provide contacts to other groups.
                                        The Author

NEWCOMERS CLUB OF BRYN MAWR

For new residents of Bryn Mawr, Haverford, Gladwyn, Villanova, Rosemont and parts of Ardmore. This group sends notices out to new residents in their area. If you think they might have missed you, you can check the local newspapers for notices of their meetings.

GREETERS-NEWCOMERS OF NEWTOWN SQUARE

For new residents in and around Newtown Square. (They are relaxed about their territory borders and welcome anyone in a 15 minute radius.) Members have many special interest groups, and a luncheon every month. Call the current president at (610) 325-9850.

NEW RESIDENTS

NEWCOMERS CLUB OF GREAT VALLEY
For new residents (3 years or less) within the Tredyffrin and Great Valley school districts. (They use the school district lines for their borders, although members do not need to have children.) Members have many special interest groups, a monthly luncheon and a coffee get-together. Call the current president at (610) 254-0142.

WELCOME WAGON CLUB OF MEDIA (NEWCOMERS CLUB)
For anyone in Delaware County; you don't even have to be a newcomer. They have monthly luncheon meetings and members also have many on-going special interest groups. Call their president at (610) 356-3333.

WELCOME WAGON CLUB OF NORTH PENN
For new residents in Lansdale, Blue Bell, North Wales, Telford, Hatfield and nearby areas. (They are relaxed about their territory borders and have had members from as far away as Collegeville.) Their rules say that you have to join within 2 years of being contacted by a Welcome Wagon hostess (this is how their flyers are distributed). If you were never contacted by a hostess you can still call. Monthly meetings are held at Pennbrook Middle School, but members also have many on-going special interest groups. Call the V.P. of membership at (215) 393-9834 or the current president at (610) 584-5193.

TOURIST INFORMATION BUREAUS

BUCKS COUNTY TOURIST COMMISSION (215) 345-4552
Doylestown, PA

CHESTER COUNTY TOURIST BUREAU (610) 344-6365
West Chester, PA

DELAWARE COUNTY TOURIST BUREAU (610) 565-3679
Media, PA

GREATER PHILA. CULTURAL ALLIANCE (215) 735-0570

MONTGOMERY COUNTY VISITORS BUREAU (610) 834-1550
(Valley Forge Convention & Visitors Bureau)

PHILA. CONVENTION & VISITORS BUREAU (215) 636-3300
1515 Market Street,
Philadelphia, PA

PHILADELPHIA VISITORS CENTER (215) 636-1666
16th Street and JFK Boulevard
Philadelphia, PA

They know everything about Philadelphia.

VISITORS CENTER (for Independence Park) (215) 597-8974
3rd and Chestnut Street
Philadelphia, PA

LOCAL SUPPORTIVE ORGANIZATIONS

PEOPLE SEEKING EMPLOYMENT

HELPFUL HINTS: If none of these organizations is suitable, it never hurts to ask if they have any alternatives to suggest. People working for these organizations usually enjoy helping people and will often go out of their way to not disappoint you. One of the best ways to maintain a sense of confidence, mental poise and contacts, while unemployed, is to immediately volunteer your skills to likely organizations. Volunteer work is flexible, can be arranged around your work search, will help you to feel valued and will keep depression and self-doubt at arms length. It will also tell prospective employers that you've got heart and motivation.

USEFUL BOOKS

THE GREATER PHILADELPHIA JOB BANK BOOK
By Bob Adams
A guide to local companies with annually revised info.

THE JOB SEEKERS GUIDE TO THE DELAWARE VALLEY
By Wendy H. Robbins & Options
A source book of local companies with detailed information.

SUPPORTIVE ORGANIZATIONS

CAREER AND COUNSELING CENTER   (610) 359-5324
Marple, PA
Part of Delaware County Community College. One of the largest self-guiding career resource centers on the East Coast. Services are free or cheap.

ENERGY FOR EMPLOYMENT   (215) 561-1660 (Hotline)
Philadelphia, PA   (Center City)
Free weekly group for job seekers; meets in Berwyn, Wayne and Telford, PA and Cherry Hill, NJ. Evaluates skills, résumé and job hunting skills.

FORTY PLUS OF PHILADELPHIA   (215) 923-2074
Philadelphia, PA
Non-profit organization offering programs and self-help support groups for job-seeking unemployed executives and professionals aged 40 and older. (South Jersey residents are welcome to participate.)

GREAT VALLEY CAREER CONNECTIONS   (610) 647-6633
Malvern, PA
Maintains a computerized résumé data base to identify ideal candidates for jobs in corporations at Great Valley Corporate Center, in Malvern, PA. Skills vary from secretarial to C.E.O. level executives. $10 processing fee.

GREATER PHIL. CULTURAL ALLIANCE   (215) 440-8100
320 Walnut Street
Philadelphia, PA   19106
Publishes a newsletter that cultural organizations advertise jobs in.

PEOPLE SEEKING EMPLOYMENT

JOB-SEARCH SUPPORT GROUP (610) 525-2821
Bryn Mawr Presbyterian Church
Bryn Mawr, PA

Free meetings at the church. Led by a professional career counselor.

LIVE AND LEARN (610) 583-9190
Project Share Consumers Center
Upper Darby, PA

Vocation oriented job-search support group. Meets once a week to discuss job-search concerns and help with résumés. Open to anyone.

LUTHERAN SETTLEMENT HOUSE (215) 426-8610
WOMEN'S PROGRAM
Philadelphia, PA

Counseling, support groups and an employment training program.

MANAGEMENT IN TRANSITION (215) 348-7453
Bucks County Library
150 South Pine Street
Doylestown, PA

"Resource network for management & professional personnel to exchange job leads, learn to market skills." Wednesdays, 7–9 pm for free.

THE MEN'S RESOURCE CENTER (610) 971-9310
Wayne, PA

Offers individual counseling, group therapy, workshops & seminars.

NEW CHOICES (at Delaware County Community College)
Marple, PA (main campus) (610) 359-5232
Chester/Collingdale, PA (off-campus center) (610) 586-5009
West Chester, PA (YWCA center) (610) 692-3737

Guidance/training programs for single parents and displaced homemakers (separated, divorced, widowed). Tuition/childcare assistance available. Sponsored by Delaware County Community College.

NEW CHOICES (at Montgomery County Community College)
Blue Bell and Norristown, PA (610) 327-3883
Pottstown, PA (215) 641-2310

Support groups, counseling, workshops, job and interview training for single parents/displaced homemakers (separated, divorced, widowed).

NEW CHOICES (at Bucks County Community College)
Adults in Transition Center
locations in Bristol and Quakertown, PA (215) 968-8188

Counseling, workshops, job and interview training, and support groups. For single parents/displaced homemakers (separated, divorced, widowed).

OPTIONS CAREER (215) 735-2202
AND HUMAN RESOURCE CONSULTING
Philadelphia, PA

Non-profit. Offers support/feedback to people interviewing for jobs. Workshops and job search support groups available. Modest fees.

LOCAL SUPPORTIVE ORGANIZATIONS

PENNSYLVANIA DEPARTMENT ON AGING (717) 783-1550
400 Market Street, State Office Building
Harrisburg, PA 17101-1195

Oversees services to seniors through area agencies.
Local Agencies for the Aging include:

Bucks County Area Agency (Doylestown)	(215) 348-0510
Chester County Office (West Chester)	(610) 344-6350
Delaware County Services (Media)	(610) 891-4455
Philadelphia Corporation for the Aging	(215) 765-9040
Montgomery County Office (Norristown)	(610) 278-3601

PROFESSIONALS IN TRANSITION
Blue Bell, PA

Self-help for professionals who are/will be seeking employment. $1 fee per meeting. Monthly meetings at 7:00 pm, 2nd and 4th Wednesdays, at Montgomery Community College in College Hall (staff dining room).

SUPPORTIVE OFFICES OF THE VARIOUS COUNTIES:

Family Service of Bucks County	(215) 757-6916
Family Service of Chester County	(610) 696-4900
Family & Social Service of Delaware County	(610) 566-7540
Family Service of Montgomery County	(610) 272-1520
Family Service of Philadelphia County	(215) 875-3300
Youth & Family Services, NJ State Hotline	1(800) 331-DYFS (Hotline)
Youth & Family Services, NJ Southern Reg.	(609) 567-0010
Catholic Social Services, Philadelphia	(215) 587-3900
Catholic Family Life Bureau, South Jersey	(609) 756-7957
Episcopal Community Services, Phila. area	(215) 351-1400
Jewish Family & Children's Service, Phila. area	(215) 545-3290
Jewish Family & Children's Service, S. NJ	(609) 662-8611
Lutheran Children & Fam. Serv. of E. PA	(215) 276-7800
Samaritan Counseling Center, PA	(215) 247-6077

Most of these organizations have offices in several locations. They should be able to refer you to other county offices or local organizations that offer job-support groups and/or retraining opportunities.

TRADESWOMEN OF PHILADELPHIA/ (215) 545-3700
WOMEN IN NON-TRADITIONAL WORK (609) 728-5931
Philadelphia, PA

A training and job placement program for women who want to enter non-traditional vocations (carpentry, plumbing, roofing, etc.). It is free to those who qualify. Call for more information.

WOMEN'S CENTER OF MONTGOMERY COUNTY

Jenkintown, PA	(610) 885-5020 (Hotline)
Norristown, PA	(610) 279-1548
Pottstown, PA	(610) 970-7363

Information and referrals, support for battered women (and protective service), job readiness training, job search support groups, legal counseling, self-help groups of various types. Some services are free and some have a fee.

PEOPLE SEEKING EMPLOYMENT

WOMEN'S OPPORTUNITY CENTER   (609) 877-4520
c/o Burlington Community College
Willingboro, NJ

A resource and information center run by the College.

WOMEN'S OPPORTUNITY   (215) 564-5500
RESOURCE CENTER
Philadelphia, PA

The organization promotes "social and economic self sufficiency for economically disadvantaged women and their children." They offer self-employment training, savings groups, and more.

THE WOMEN'S RESOURCE CENTER   (610) 687-6391
113 West Wayne Avenue   Mon.–Thurs. 9:30–3:00
P.O. Box 309
Wayne, PA 19087

A non-profit organization. Over the phone they'll give referrals, suggestions and contacts to non-members and members. On site they offer workshops; free drop-in counseling; free legal consultations; and support groups for divorce, career, divorce finanical issues, and for single mothers (free). There is a reference library. They also have a mid-life group that meets for brunch, a social group that meets for dinners and much more. Sliding scale rates may be available. Memb. $25/yr. (includes a monthly newsletter and discounts for activities.)

WORKPLACE   (215) 686-5436
Job and Career Info. Center for Adults
The Free Library of Philadelphia
Logan Square, PA
and
Chester County Library   (610) 363-0884
Exton, PA

Designed to help adults assess their skills and knowledge, and identify steps toward career goals. Offers periodicals and directories, computer vocational tests, financial aid information, word processing programs for résumés, useful videotapes, workshops, referrals to other helpful agencies, and résumé critiquing. Most services are free.

YWCA RESOURCE CENTER   (609) 435-6606
DISPLACED HOMEMAKER PROGRAM
Camden County, NJ

Specifically for single females in Camden County. They do personal counseling, career assessment and more.

LOCAL SUPPORTIVE ORGANIZATIONS   Page 117

RETIRED / OLDER ADULTS / SENIORS

HOTLINES

Contact Philadelphia   (215) 879-4402
Counseling and Crisis Hotline
Hopeline for the troubled, deaf and elderly. Volunteers remain anonymous as they listen and give emotional support, and assist callers with problem solving.

First Call for help (United Way)   (215) 568-3750
Supports all sorts of social and community services, and can refer you to the one closest to your needs.

Mayor's Commission on Aging   (215) 686-3504/3505

National Council on Aging   1(800) 424-9046

ADVICE AND SUPPORT SERVICES

HELPFUL HINTS   Many of the organizations listed have printed books (available for free) listing *mountains* of resource information. They'll be happy to tell you about all of the other groups I haven't mentioned, and you'll be overwhelmed in no time. If you want to find meetings or activities for older citizens, try buying the Sunday Inquirer and look for the community "Bulletin Board" page. It will list meetings of hobby groups, clubs, support groups and organizations in your area.

ACTION ALLIANCE OF SENIOR CITIZENS   (215) 574-8520
Philadelphia, PA
Free info., referral, technical and legal assistance. From a coalition of over 300 Senior Citizen's clubs. Call for info. on joining member clubs.

AMERICAN ASSOC. OF RETIRED PERSONS "AARP"
225 Market St., Suite 502   (717) 238-2277
Harrisburg, PA 17101
or,
To reach the Philadelphia Chapter contact: (215) 765-9040
There are local groups of members that meet on a regular basis (usually at libraries). Offers benefits, programs, discounts to members, a magazine about retirement issues, and more. Call the State office for information about groups outside of Philadelphia.

C.A.R.I.E.   (215) 545-5728
Coalition of Advocates for the Rights   (215) 545-4437 (Hotline)
of the Infirm Elderly
Philadelphia, PA
For seniors and their families. Helps with caregiver resources, legal problems, and legislation.

RETIRED / OLDER ADULTS / SENIORS

CONTACT PHILADELPHIA, INC.   (215) 877-9099

Free. Volunteers offer telephone reassurance and can call, at prearranged times, to check on and converse with elderly/homebound persons (or start emergency procedures if there is no reply).

COUNSELING AND SUPPORT GROUPS FOR ALL AGES

Family Service of Bucks County	(215) 757-6916
Family Service of Chester County	(610) 696-4900
Family & Social Service of Delaware County	(610) 566-7540
Family Service of Montgomery County	(610) 272-1520
Family Service of Philadelphia County	(215) 875-3300
Youth & Family Services, NJ State Hotline	1(800) 331-DYFS (Hotline)
Youth & Family Services, NJ Southern Reg.	(609) 567-0010
Catholic Social Services, Philadelphia	(215) 587-3900
Catholic Family Life Bureau, South Jersey	(609) 756-7957
Episcopal Community Services, Phila. area	(215) 351-1400
Jewish Family & Children's Service, Phila. area	(215) 545-3290
Jewish Family & Children's Service, S. NJ	(609) 662-8611
Lutheran Children & Fam. Serv. of E. PA	(215) 276-7800
Samaritan Counseling Center, PA	(215) 247-6077

Many of these organizations have offices in several locations. Most offer all types of support groups, individual counseling and lend their facilities to a variety of support organizations for meetings. The religious organizations offer many things that the County Services do, but they also have groups that have religion in common. Usually, their counselors have been trained in psychology. Samaritan Counseling Center is in 8 areas, is inter-religious and doesn't discuss religion unless you do.

LOWER MERION-NARBERTH   (610) 525-0706
COALITION ON AGING AND ADULT SERVICES
Bryn Mawr, PA

The Coalition says that it "helps older people and their families with transportation, shopping, visitors, odd jobs, volunteer opportunities and information." They offer a free daily telephone check-up service. They can also give you referral information about other agencies.

NATIONAL SELF-HELP CLEARING HOUSE   (212) 354-8525
New York, NY

Will match you with the support group that you need, locally or nationally. Possibilities include groups seeking leads for rare disorders, self-help for anorexics or endometriosis patients, support for the very short or tall, and computer groups for the homebound. Based in Manhattan.

NEWSPAPERS FOR OLDER ADULTS

There are two that are free when they are distributed to stores in the area. One is called <u>Vintage Magazine</u>—the other is <u>The Golden Times</u>. <u>Vintage Magazine</u> has personal ads in the back. <u>The Golden Times</u> has a "Bulletin Board" section that lists everthing from Square dances, to a "Zoo Senior Group" that meets at the Zoo. They are both listed under "Useful Local Publications" in the *Other Resources* section. You can also subscribe to them.

LOCAL SUPPORTIVE ORGANIZATIONS

PENNSYLVANIA DEPARTMENT ON AGING   (717) 783-1550
400 Market Street, State Office Building
Harrisburg, PA 17101-1195

Oversees services to seniors through area agencies. The agencies, in turn, oversee and evaluate senior services such as health care, adult day care, volunteer opportunity services, legal aid, employment and job training opportunities, homemaker services, advocacy and social services. They are a reference service as well and can advise you on which other departments to contact for specific needs. Many services are free.
Local **Agencies for the Aging include:**

Bucks County Area Agency (Doylestown)	(215) 348-0510
Chester County Office (West Chester)	(610) 344-6350
Delaware County Services (Media)	(610) 891-4455
Philadelphia Corporation for the Aging	(215) 765-9040
Montgomery County Office (Norristown)	(610) 278-3601

SENIOR CENTERS

You can find them listed in the phone book, usually in the blue pages under the "Older Adults-Senior Citizens" category. They often announce their weekly activities in local newspapers and in the Neighbors Bulletin Board section of the Sunday Philadelphia Inquirer. They often have bus trip outings to museums, sports games and theater performances. On location, they often have leagues for bridge and other games, lectures, socials and many types of activities.

THE YM & YWCA

Originally "Young Christian Associations" for men and women, these organizations are now co-ed, with members from every religion and age group. They offer everything from swimming lessons for babies to activity oriented support groups. They often have social and activity groups that are specifically for older adults. You will find them in the phone book.

THE YM & YWHA

Originally "Young Hebrew Associations" for men and women, they now offer completely non-sectarian activities for people of all ages along with activities for Jewish members. They are just as likely to attract a mixed crowd for volleyball as they are to offer Israeli folk dancing. They often offer groups and activities that are meant for older adults. Now a part of a much bigger organization, the YM & YWHAs in this area are also Jewish Community Centers (JCCs). You will find them listed under Jewish Community Centers in the phone book.

JEWISH COMMUNITY CENTERS (JCCs)

See the description for YM & YWHA

NOTES

OTHER RESOURCES

In and Around
PHILADELPHIA

USEFUL HOT LINES / PHONE NUMBERS / MISC.

HELPFUL HINTS: Most emergency or community service numbers can be found in your local Yellow Pages, or in the blue page section of your local White Pages.

LOCAL HOTLINES

Consumer Protection Hotline	1(800) 441-2555 (Hotline)
Governor's Action Center	1(800) 932-0784 (Hotline)
Mayor's Action Center	(215) 686-3000 (Hotline)
Philadelphia Weather	(215) 936-1212 (Hotline)
Stamps by Phone	1(800) STAMP-24

U.S. Postal Service. There is a $3 service charge or more (depending on how much you order).

Time	(215) 846-1212 (Hotline)
Zip Code Information	(215) 895-9000 (Hotline)

USEFUL NATIONAL HOTLINES

Federal Information Center   1(800) 347-1997
Philadelphia, PA

The only Federal office that is specially trained to help you sort out all of the other Federal departments and divisions. They'll listen to your problem and tell you which government department to contact.

LOCAL RECYCLING INFORMATION:

Recycling Hotline (weekdays 9–5 pm)   1(800) 346-4242

This office can refer you to local recycling phone numbers if the phone numbers below don't suit your purpose.

Bucks County	(215) 345-3400
Chester County	(610) 344-5940
Delaware County	(610) 892-9627
Montgomery County	(610) 278-3618
Philadelphia County	1(800) 80-RECYCLE
Pennsylvania Resources Council	(610) 353-1555

HOW TO VISIT NYC CHEAPLY

Take the R7 SEPTA train (from 30th St., Suburban or Market East stations) to Trenton and then take a New Jersey Transit train into New York City (Penn Station). It's cheapest to buy round trip SEPTA tickets in

PA as you leave and the NJ Transit tickets when you first arrive in Trenton. Buy from the ticket office/ticket machine if possible; it costs more to purchase tickets on the train. Either way, it's dramatically less expensive than Amtrak. If you ask about connection times for the trains, you'll have time to race to the ticket office in Trenton and still catch the connection train waiting to leave for New York.

USEFUL LOCAL PUBLICATIONS

ADVERTISING COMMUNICATION TIMES (215) 629-1666
121 Chestnut Street
Philadelphia, PA 19106

1 yr. subscription $39. Favorite newspaper for anyone in the advertising industry or public relations.

ART MATTERS (215) 564-2340
101 Greenwood Avenue, Suite 130
Jenkintown, PA 19046

Devoted to articles about art; it lists Delaware Valley gallery showings and exhibition opportunities for artists. Free copies can be found at art related locations. 1 yr. subscription $19.50.

BUSINESS PHILADELPHIA (215) 735-6969
Geographic Business Publishers Inc.
The Atlantic Bldg.
260 S. Broad Street
Philadelphia, PA 19102

Subscription is $32.50/yr. Articles about local businesses. Each month emphasizes something different (often with a resource list).

CITY PAPER (215) 735-8444
206 South 13th Street
Philadelphia, PA 19107

One of Philadelphia's free weekly newspapers. Lists: concerts, comedy clubs, dance events, galleries, movies, theater events, and has personal ads. Free copies available in vending machines all over Philadelphia.

DANCE! Magazine
Mr. Ed Armon, 317 Dalton Street
Philadelphia, PA 19111-1802

A magazine that lists all of the square dance clubs in the Delaware Valley and surrounding area. Special dance events are also listed. A subscription is $11.50/yr. (10 issues per year).

DELAWARE COUNTY MAGAZINE (610) 565-3679
Delaware County Convention and Visitors Bureau
200 E. State Street, Suite 100
Media, PA 19063

1 yr. subscription $6. Full color magazine with listings of special events, museums and house tours. Free at various locations.

Page 124 USEFUL HOT LINES / PHONE NUMBERS / MISC.

DELAWARE TODAY (302) 656-1809
201 North Walnut St., Suite 1204   1(800) 285-0400
Wilmington, DE 19801

Delaware's answer to Philadelphia Magazine. Has articles about local people, personal ads and lists local events. Subscription $18/yr.

DELAWARE VALLEY COMPUTER USER   (302) 454-8511
256 Chapman Rd., Oxford Bldg., Suite 104
Newark, DE 19702

Articles on software, hardware, User Groups and Computer Bulletin Boards. Subscription $12. Free copies are at stores all around Philly.

THE GOLDEN TIMES   (609) 582-3940
P.O. Box 134
Pitman, NJ 08071

"The Delaware Valley newspaper for active residents over age 55." The back of the paper lists events, dances and courses that are specifically for older adults. $10/yr. sub. Free copies are at area stores.

THE GREATER PHILADELPHIA SENIOR CITIZEN RESOURCE DIRECTORY
Philadelphia County Medical Society
2100 Spring Garden Street
Philadelphia, PA 19130

Free, published yearly. Found in CoreStates Banks all around Philly.

LABYRINTH   (215) 724-6181
The Philadelphia Women's Newspaper
4722 Baltimore Avenue
Philadelphia, PA 19143

A feminist publication. "Seeks to promote understanding among women of different races, classes, and sexual orientation."

MAIN LINE MAGAZINE   (610) 995-9600
237 Lancaster Avenue, Suite 150
Devon, PA 19333

Monthly articles about people/places in the area. Distributed free to some Main Line locations and sold at various Main Line stores. $12/1 yr.

MAIN LINE SCHOOL NIGHT ASSOC.   (610) 687-0460
260 Gulph Creek Road, P.O. Box 8175
Radnor, PA 19087-9175

Has a 96-page booklet of very inexpensive, very popular, 1–5 week courses given at 5 locations on the Main Line. Classes range from cooking to care repair. Distributed free along the Main Line (to libraries for example). Can be picked up in person; they won't mail them.

METROKIDS MAGAZINE   (215) 551-3200
KidStuff Publications, Inc.
Riverview Plaza, 1400 S. Columbus Blvd.
Philadelphia, PA 19147-5526

1 yr. subscription $15. Free copies are distributed to stores around the area. Subtitled "The resource for parents and children in the Delaware Valley." One issue I saw had 9 pages of events for children.

OTHER RESOURCES

NEW JERSEY MONTHLY   1(800) 669-1002
P.O. Box 1962
Marion, OH 43302-1962

Slick and well done. Lists events and divides them into North, Central and South Jersey categories. Has personals in the back. Editorial offices are in Morristown. 1 yr. subscription/$19.95.

**OLDER ADULTS GUIDE FOR SERVICES
IN MONTGOMERY COUNTY**

A paperback book. Available from the Montgomery County Aging and Adult Services (610) 278-3601/ (610) 527-7962, or from the Lower Merion-Narberth Coalition on Aging and Adult Services (610) 525-0706.

OLDER PENNSYLVANIANS HANDBOOK   (717) 783-7247
A GUIDE TO BENEFITS AND RIGHTS
Pennsylvania Department of Aging
231 State Street
Harrisburg, PA 17101-1195

A wonderful book that offers information on everything from food stamps to Alzheimer's Disease.

ON THE AIR MAGAZINE   1(800) 473-2224
P.O. Box 19600
Denver, CO 80219

1 yr. subscription/approx. $20. Monthly magazine for WFLN, Philadelphia's classical music station. Lists program schedules for the entire month. Sold in some bookstores.

PARENT'S EXPRESS   (215) 629-1774
P.O. Box 12900
Philadelphia, PA 19108

1 yr. subscription $12. Free copies are distributed to stores around the area. Contains articles on child and parent issues.

PARENT'S GUIDE OF DELAWARE VALLEY   (215) 343-8400
P.O. Box 308   (609) 835-4554
Warrington, PA 18976

1 yr. subscription $12. Free copies are distributed to stores around the area. Has articles about kid/parent issues and a monthly calendar of activities. Lists workshops and resource organizations for parents.

PENNSYLVANIA ANGLER
Pennsylvania Fish & Boat Commission
3532 Walnut Street
Harrisburg, PA 17109

$9 for a 1 yr. subscription. Self-described as "The Keystone State's official fishing magazine."

THE PENNSYLVANIA BAR ASSOCIATION
P.O. Box 186
Harrisburg, PA 17108

Pamphlets on specific topics (lawyers and fees, divorce, making a will, etc.) are available without charge and are often found at libraries.

USEFUL HOT LINES / PHONE NUMBERS / MISC.

PENNSYLVANIA FOLKLIFE
P.O. Box 92
Collegeville, PA 19426

Published 3 times a year by the Penn. Folklife Society. $15 for a 1 yr. subscription. Each issue covers a particular part of Pennsylvania history (The Amish for example). Has lovely photos and a schedule of folklife events (festivals and Historical Societies for example).

PENNSYLVANIA GAME & FISH
Circulation and Fulfillment Center
P.O. Box 741
Marietta, GA 30061-9973

1 yr. subscription $14.95. The title pretty much says it all. A fairly slick magazine with photos and articles. I've seen it for sale in bookstores.

PENNSYLVANIA GAME NEWS
2001 Elmerton Ave.
Harrisburg, PA 17110-9797

Published by the Pennsylvania Game Commission. $9 for a 1 yr. subscription. The title pretty much says it all.

PENNSYLVANIA GOLFER   (610) 269-7670
18 Webb Road
Downingtown, PA 19335

A magazine that is often available for free at local public golf courses, it lists events and golf news for the area. A subscription is $7/yr.

PENNSYLVANIA MAGAZINE   1(800) 537-2624
P.O. Box 576
Camp Hill, PA 17001-0576

1 yr. subscription/$18.95. Covers historical and crafts topics. Lists fairs, antique and crafts shows, etc. all over Pennsylvania.

PENNSYLVANIA SPORTSMAN
Northwoods Publications, Inc.
P.O. Box 90
Lemoyne, PA 17043-9954

1 yr. subscription/$16.97. Slick magazine with articles on hunting, etc.

PHILADELPHIA BUSINESS JOURNAL   (215) 238-1450
and **SOUTH JERSEY BUSINESS JOURNAL**
400 Market Street, Suite 300
Philadelphia, PA 19106

Two weekly newspapers that specialize in annual listings of things like "Largest Area Shopping Malls" (with lease information). Inside, they list meetings and seminars of various local business groups. They also issue yearly booklets describing major corporations in the area.

THE PHILADELPHIA DAILY NEWS   (215) 854-2000
400 N. Broad St.
Philadelphia, PA 19101

Philadelphia's 2nd largest newspaper. It's owned by the same people who own the Philadelphia Inquirer and is in the same building (with the same

OTHER RESOURCES

phone number). The <u>Daily News</u> is targeted toward the common man in contrast to the <u>Inquirer</u>'s more intellectual approach.

PHILADELPHIA GAY NEWS   (215) 625-8501
254 South 11th Street
Philadelphia, PA 19107

A newspaper/magazine for alternative lifestyles.

PHILADELPHIA GOLFER   (215) 568-GOLF
290 Commerce Drive
Fort Washington, PA 19034

A monthly golf newspaper/magazine. Covers local golf play and courses. Often free at public courses. A 1 yr. subscription is $19.95.

THE PHILADELPHIA INQUIRER   (215) 854-2000
400 N. Broad St.
Philadelphia, PA 19101

Philadelphia's most respected, serious newspaper. The Friday edition "Weekend" magazine lists a particularly large variety of special events just before holidays. The "Neighbors" section of the Sunday edition covers just about everything else. Read them for: museums, galleries, special performances, concerts, movies, sports, family events, nightlife, auditions, beach, ski and fishing conditions, and support group meetings.

PHILADELPHIA MAGAZINE   (215) 564-7700
1818 Walnut Street   1(800) 777-1003
Philadelphia, PA 19103-3683

1 yr. subscription $15. Contains a list of monthly events, theater and music performances, restaurant information and local trivia. Feature articles discuss hot scandals, politics and high society. The personal ads at the back are the most respected in the area. Widely sold.

PHILADELPHIA WEEKLY   (215) 563-7400
1701 Walnut Street
Philadelphia, PA 19103-5222

A free weekly newspaper for the creative side of Philly. Lists artsy events (folk dancing, small budget theater, local theater and choral auditions, poetry readings, etc.). Has a large real estate and apartment rental section and personal ads. Distributed free all over Philly and found on street corners in vending machines.

PROFESSIONAL SINGLES NETWORK MAG.   (215) 878-0200
Bala Cynwyd, PA

A magazine for personal ads of local "upscale, educated singles."

RELOCATION QUARTERLY   (215) 321-3210
1075-4 River Rd.
P.O. Box 508
Washington Crossing, PA 18977-0508

A quarterly newspaper for potential homebuyers. It lists everything from school district S.A.T. scores to the tax rate of local communities. Free copies are often available at libraries. A subscription is $20/yr.

USEFUL HOT LINES / PHONE NUMBERS / MISC.

SINGLES AT THE SHORE (609) 272-8677
203 Seville Avenue
West Atlantic City, NJ 08232

Free at the Jersey Shore. Free personal ads and an activity list.

SINGLES MAGAZINE (609) 778-7787
560 Fellowship Road
Mount Laurel, NJ 08054

Free in Jersey and Philly. Contains free personal ads and an activity list.

THE SINGLES REGISTER (610) 353-4624
Professional Business Singles Network
Box 404
Paoli, PA 19301

1 yr. subscription/$12. A magazine listing PBSN singles activities, and personal ads. You do not have to join or subscribe to attend events. Call and ask to receive a trial copy of the magazine; this will let you try out the large variety of events offered.

SNOWDRIFTS

Published by the Eastern Pennsylvania Ski Council, which is made up of all the ski clubs in the area. It lists who to contact from each club and lists Ski Council activities. Free, every autumn and spring, at ski shops.

STAGE (610) 565-2094
9 East Rose Valley Road
Wallingford, PA 19086

1 yr. subscription/$9. A publication of the Eastern Pa. Theater Council. This monthly booklet lists performances/auditions of community theater groups and professional theater groups all over the Delaware Valley.

VINTAGE MAGAZINE (610) 664-4066
1 Bala Plaza, Suite 619
Bala Cynwyd, PA 19004

"For active mature adults." More a newspaper than magazine; there are articles and personal ads for the 50-plus crowd. Subscription $12/yr. Free copies are distributed to shops and stores.

VISIONS MAGAZINE (215) 249-9190
24 Kern Drive
Perkasie, PA 18944

Features a Delaware Valley holistic resource directory. Category examples include: Alexander Technique, natural restaurants, Reflexology, health food stores and Acupuncture. Free at health food stores.

USEFUL LOCAL BOOKS

HELPFUL HINTS: Don't forget to look at the "Local Interest" shelves of your local bookstores. New publications crop up and there are books on local childcare information, golf and outdoor activities in Pennsylvania that I haven't mentioned. Philadelphia also has many books on historic subjects by local authors.

OTHER RESOURCES

CONNECTING IN PHILADELPHIA
By Ruth Harvey $9.95
Offtime Press

The author teaches seminars for singles in Philadelphia.

FIFTY HIKES IN EASTERN PENNSYLVANIA
By Carolyn Hoffman, Backcountry Publications
P.O. Box 175   *$12.00 in stores.*
Woodstock, VT 05091

THE GREATER PHILADELPHIA JOB BANK   1(800) USA-JOBS
Bob Adams, Inc.
260 Center Street   *$15.95 in stores.*
Holbrook, MA 02343

Includes detailed information on all major area employers. Tells you who to call, where to write, and what to say. Available at some libraries.

GUIDE TO JEWISH PHILADELPHIA   (215) 893-5821
Jewish Information & Referral Service
226 South 16th Street
Philadelphia, PA 19102-3391

Guidebook that lists everything from cultural programs to day care to Kosher establishments. Call to order it.

THE JOB SEEKER'S GUIDE   *$11.95 in stores.*
TO THE DELAWARE VALLEY
By Wendy Robbins & Options, Inc., Camino Books
P.O. Box 59026
Philadelphia, PA 19102

A listing of employers and job-seeking tips in the Delaware Valley.

THE PARENTS GUIDE TO THE DELAWARE VALLEY
by Cynthia Roberts, Camino Books
P.O. Box 59026   *$12.95 in stores.*
Philadelphia, PA 19102

A resource guide to children's healthcare facilities, adoption, childcare, schools, culture, parks, party places and more.

PHILADELPHIA WITH CHILDREN   (202) 686-6703
Gephardt and Cunningham, Starrhill Press
P.O. Box 32342   *$11.95 in stores.*
Washington, DC 20007

PLACES TO GO WITH CHILDREN IN THE DELAWARE VALLEY
by Alice Rowan O'Brien, Chronicle Books
275 5th Street   *$9.95 in stores.*
San Francisco, CA 94103

Has locations of places to take kids and an events calendar.

THE THRIFT SHOP MANIAC'S GUIDED TOUR   (215) 635-4208
P.O. Box 27540   (215) 635-4208 Fax
Philadelphia, PA 19118-0448   *$12.95 in stores*

Lists and describes thrift shops and used item consignment stores.

Page 130   USEFUL HOT LINES / PHONE NUMBERS / MISC.

25 BICYCLE TOURS IN EASTERN PENNSYLVANIA
By Adams and Speicher, Backcountry Publications
P.O. Box 175   *$10.00 in stores.*
Woodstock, VT   05091

THE WOMEN'S YELLOW PAGES   (610) 446-4747
P.O. Box 1002
Havertown, PA   19083   *$4.95 in stores*

A Delaware Valley resource guide. All the business listings are either owned by or are supportive of women. In bookstores and at libraries.

ZAGAT SURVEY   (212) 977-6000
OF PHILADELPHIA RESTAURANTS
4 Columbus Circle
New York, NY   10019

Annual restaurant guide (includes S. Jersey, Jersey Shore, Wilmington).

USEFUL NATIONAL PUBLICATIONS

| HELPFUL HINTS: | Many of these may be at your local library.

DIAL AN EXPERT
by Susan Osborn, McGraw-Hill Publication

"Consumer's sourcebook of free/low-cost expertise available by phone."

GALES ENCYCLOPEDIA OF ASSOCIATIONS
Gale Research Corp. of Detroit

A set of volumes listing 15,000 registered Associations in the U.S. Only the main headquarters office of each group is listed, and so you must contact them for information about local chapters. (Ask if they hold meetings or just have a newsletter.) Listings range from archery, to politics, to the arts. Available at most public libraries. (Don't bother looking at state or city volumes; the entries are dismal.)

MATTHEW LESKO BOOKS: (301) 369-1519
Information USA, Inc.
P.O. Box E
Kensington, MD   20895

Lesko has several very large books that are often found at libraries. Info-Power lists 30,000 sources that either offer free information or financial aid in some way, shape or form. The categories include "Free Help In Finding Free Experts," "Career and Job Training Opportunities" and "1,000 Money programs for Homeowners, Investors, Students, Inventors, Researchers and Artists." Among his other books are: What to do when you can't afford health care, and Government give-aways for entrepreneurs. The books each cost approximately $34.

STANDARD RATE AND DATA SERVICES

A book that lists 75,000 mailing lists available for purchase. Can be found at the University of Pennsylvania Library. Call first to check availability at other libraries.

OTHER RESOURCES

SUGGESTED READING

HELPFUL HINTS: These are books I have found to be very helpful in life.

GETTING THE LOVE YOU WANT
by Harville Hendrix, Ph.D.
Published by Harper & Row

A book that can help readers understand why a relationship that began well might be going sour—and how it might get back on track. According to the author, people often fall in love with those who display the very emotional traits they themselves are afraid to reveal. First they admire it; then they find themselves tempted to emulate their partner but terrified to do so. Eventually they find that the very things they once admired about their partner now annoy and upset them. Hendrix feels that the whole point is to overcome those fears and that, if both partners can do so, they'll have the most satisfying relationship they've ever encountered and learn from each other. He suggests ways to achieve this.

WISHCRAFT
How to Get What You Really Want
By Barbara Sher
Published by Ballantine

Sher points out that it's very hard to accomplish anything in life entirely on your own without a supportive group of unbiased friends around you. Family members have too much self interest to be truly unbiased. She advocates creating a support team in which the members meet regularly and keep each other going—through thick and thin.

REBUILDING
When Your Relationship Ends
By Bruce Fisher
Published by Impact Publishers

When I told a girlfriend I was getting divorced she sent me this book and it became my Bible. The author explains the stages we all go through when we experience loss/divorce and he explains them exceptionally well. There is a chapter for each stage, and it's satisfying to think, "Aha, I've managed to move to the next chapter—I'm in the next stage!" It's also nice to peek ahead and see where you are headed. It manages to give you some sense of control over a very difficult and confusing process.

HOW TO WORK THE COMPETITION INTO THE GROUND
& HAVE FUN DOING IT!
By John T. Malloy

A rather alarming title for a very helpful and very interesting book. Malloy is a research specialist who decided to research people's working habits. He categorizes the results. You decide which category you fit into and read how *your* particular category can work more efficiently on the job or at home. He gives examples and tells entertaining stories. If you take it seriously, you can become more productive, yet create more free time for yourself.

Page 132   **USEFUL HOT LINES / PHONE NUMBERS / MISC.**

TIPS: HOW TO WRITE / ANSWER A PERSONAL AD

Despite common feelings of reluctance to try them, personal ads can be a good way to meet intelligent, educated, desirable people. I met my former husband (a handsome, athletic, M.B.A.) when he answered a personal ad of mine and I know of other couples who met in the same way. My marriage didn't work, but it had nothing to do with the ad. I did eventually try the personals again. I didn't meet a mate the second time, but I did meet some extremely nice men who became friends!

If you meet someone at a party you might date them for weeks before discovering that they don't want children, or have no desire to marry again. These are usually taboo topics with a new acquaintance. The advantage of the personals is that you can both put your cards on the table and cover topics closest to your heart within the first phone conversation (or meeting over a cup of coffee). *Only then*, do you decide if you want to date each other. The people you meet from personal ads tend to be serious about looking for a true relationship and are quite open about it.

However, every time I encourage a friend to write a personal ad they panic and say "I don't know what to write." And indeed, a lot of the personal ads that do end up in print are singularly un-inspiring to read.

This is my suggestion for writing an ad, (it's how I did it and since one magazine ended up promoting my ad as their "Mate of the Month," I must have done something right):

Read the personal ads for a few weeks. When you see one that you sincerely wish you had written, *tear it out and keep it*. Once you have several ads, copy the sentences that you particularly liked from each ad, onto a notepad. Next, try and rewrite each sentence to refer to yourself instead. Then piece the sentences together and add in any information that is missing. For example, I picked an ad in which a woman said she had "Green eyes, a warm laugh and freckles." I felt it communicated an unaffected attractiveness. I wanted to mention that I was pretty but add more depth to it, and so I wrote, "Pretty with warm smile and laugh" in my own ad.

The same woman also wrote "Seeks male 30–45. He is courageous, kind, has an open heart for my wonderful 6 year old son, knows there are many options and alternatives in life and knows how to treat a special relationship." Now I ask you, wouldn't you be more likely to answer an ad like that than one that said, "Seeks male 30–45, non-smoker, professional and wealthy, to go to the movies, theater and restaurants with?" The most effective ads are the ones that communicate *qualities, as well as* the things you want to share. They show heart. I also liked the way one of the male advertisers approached a touchy subject. He wrote, "Letter and photograph please, but I will reciprocate if requested" which made it seem a bit less demanding and one sided.

OTHER RESOURCES

As far as answering ads goes, I have some definite advice:

Do not write, "Hi, I really liked your ad, call and tell me more about yourself" on an office memo pad and expect a response. The person who placed the ad has just spent time and money on an ad that has already revealed quite a lot. They are not going to reveal any more until they hear something about YOU first. But don't go to the opposite extreme and send 5 pages of single spaced typewritten information about yourself. And xeroxed form response letters are a bad idea, because they seem very unfeeling, businesslike and impersonal.

What I suggest is that you create a generic response letter that you are happy with and can adapt for an individual response. Start out by mentioning something you liked about the person's ad. Then go into your generic letter (a pre-written description of yourself and what you are looking for). End with more comments or questions about the ad. If the person has asked for a photo, then you really should send a photo or a xerox of one. It makes a big difference. And also remember, if you are nervous about such things, that you can mail the response with only your first name and phone number in it.

Do not be afraid to answer more than one ad at a time. The larger the number of people you come in contact with, the greater your chances will be of meeting someone compatible. If you send out 6 responses a month, you will probably get one or two replies a month. **Remember, this is a form of personal marketing**! Even JC Penney doesn't expect to get an order from every single person they mail a catalog to!

Clip out the ads you answered and keep them beside the phone (taped to a piece of paper). This way, if you receive a response by phone, you can tactfully say, "Just refresh my memory and repeat a bit of your ad for me. I have the magazine right here beside me so I can look it up." **Avoid** saying things like, "I'm afraid I don't remember your ad."

If the two of you do decide to get together and meet, pick a public spot that is easy for both of you to get to. Give each other a description of the clothes you will be wearing. Meet for coffee rather than lunch or dinner. If things go well you can *always* extend it but it's hard to do the reverse.

If you *don't* hit it off and you end up feeling that you have less in common than you originally thought, **be honest and say so** at the end of the meeting. It is also perfectly acceptable to say, "It was really nice to meet you, I enjoyed our conversation, but to tell you the truth I simply don't feel as though you are my type." Or to say, "You know, I have a friend who would be a much better match for you than I am." (This is how I ended up introducing one of my girlfriends to the man who is now her husband.) But in any case, remember to wish each other the best of luck when you part.

Have Fun!

ABOUT PERSONAL ADS AND DATING SERVICES

WHERE THE PERSONAL ADS ARE FOUND:

The cost of placing a personal ad varies enormously. It can range from free, to $30 for a complete paragraph in a smaller publication, to the cost of an ad in Philadelphia Magazine (a few dollars per word). On one hand, a large, fairly sophisticated audience reads Philadelphia Magazine, which might mean that the investment is worth it to you. On the other hand, you might be able to put ads into several other publications for what it costs you to place just one ad in Philadelphia Magazine. Or, you might decide that the most economical route is to respond to other people's ads. In this case you should check out every publication you come across.

Publications I have noticed that run personal ads (some are free) include:
The Inquirer, The Daily News, The City Paper, Philadelphia Weekly, Philadelphia Magazine, New Jersey Monthly, The Singles Register, Professional Singles Network and very many small/local suburban newspapers.

SPECIAL INTEREST PERSONALS

There are ads for these in publications like Philadelphia Magazine (usually intermingled with the personal ads). They are called things like: The Art Lovers Exchange, The Classical Music Lovers Exchange, Single Booklovers, The Right Stuff, etc. Some have a good sucess rate!

These are often semi-club organizations in which you pay a membership fee (such as $45), fill out a profile questionnaire and write a personal ad. Your personal ad is then displayed in a monthly newsletter for a specific period of time. In some cases people will respond to your ad by mailing a letter to the club (the club forwards it to you). In other cases they may write to the club asking to see a print-out copy of your profile—and *then* send you a response directly or via the club mailing address.

ABOUT DATING SERVICES

These are usually much more expensive than personal ads, but many people use them for a variety of reasons. Some because they feel it saves them time; some because they hope the dating service will do a better job at finding people they are compatible with than they themselves have done. Others reason that they are likely to meet people from a similar income bracket or background.

The prices of these services can vary enormously from fairly expensive to extremely expensive, but none of them are cheap. You must look on the whole thing as an investment for your future if you decide to try any of them. Dating services often advertise in the yellow pages. They also advertise in magazines or newspapers that carry personal ads (usually intermingled with the personal ads).

OTHER RESOURCES

VIDEO DATING SERVICES

These definitely work for some people. I have heard from 2 sources that the percentage of men who register with video dating services tends to be slightly higher than women, which is unusual. As a client, you would be interviewed on videotape and have photos of you placed in a viewing book. After that, you would be expected to turn up at the office regularly and sift through the viewing books to look at information and photos of other clients. If you saw someone you liked, you would ask to see their videotape. If you still liked what you saw, you would leave an official note asking them to view your own videotape. Once they had done so, if they wanted to meet you they would be put in contact with you. The rest would be up to you and fate. There are often several levels of membership (all of them expensive); the top one gives you access to client books at every branch the dating service has in the area or nationally. The cheapest membership is usually valid only at the branch you register at. *Warning! Usually, you must also pay for the photos for the viewing book and these must be taken by THEIR photographer. They may let you supplement these with a favorite photo of your own.*

A friend of mine tried a video dating service. She concluded that the potential was quite good. Though she was limited to dating men from the branch she registered at, searching through their client books was a fairly overwhelming task (they get updated regularly). But she herself was overweight, and the response to her video tape was disappointing. So perhaps a dating method that put less immediate emphasis on appearance would have been better for her. I myself interviewed the manager of a videotape dating service on the phone once. She struck me as quite straight forward and stated that only a very few clients were in their 20's, a large number of their clients were 40 and up, but that the great majority were in their 30's. By her observations, she also stated that appearance made more difference than age and that many men didn't seem to care if a female was older than they were.

MATCHMAKING SERVICES

Matchmakers and Dating Services have varying methods, styles, backgrounds and prices but are always very expensive (several thousand dollars is typical). In return they usually guarantee a specific number of introductions.

I have a friend who became a matchmaker. He was a corporate headhunter originally. Now, instead of being hired by corporations that want him to search the world for the perfect employee, he is hired by people who want him to search the world for a compatible mate. Both careers have a lot in common with that of a private detective, with elements of a psychologist mixed in as well. Matchmakers are often hired by people who are either tired of looking or who simply don't have the time to look for a mate. I have a girlfriend who fit this description and used a matchmaker at one point.

ABOUT PERSONAL ADS AND DATING SERVICES

A matchmaker will first listen to your description of what you are looking for and then set up a couple of blind dates for you. Afterwards, they will interview you to find out if they are on the right track or not. By this method they determine what it is that you are REALLY looking for and subsequent dates usually get closer and closer to the mark. The people they introduce you to will usually have come to their attention through a variety of methods. One might be a client registered with them; another might have made their acquaintance at some public function. A third might have been recommended by friends of the matchmaker, and a fourth might have answered an ad that the matchmaker placed. In other words, matchmakers are paid to do the footwork and screening that you don't want to do.

In order for this method to work, you must be the type of person who is willing to open up and talk about feelings. If you are an intensely private person you will resent being prodded to reveal yourself.

If you can't get a matchmaker recommended to you (not uncommon, since many people are too embarrassed to tell their friends), ask the matchmaker for references and find out as much as you can beforehand.

SPECIAL EVENTS/ SEASONAL EVENTS

In and Around
PHILADELPHIA

SUMMER HANGOUTS

> **HELPFUL HINTS:** Those of you new to the area may wonder why the Delaware Valley seems so deserted on weekends. This is because East Coast residents migrate towards water when the weather hits 75 degrees. The desire to escape the inland heat is such that singles gather together as a group so they can afford to rent a large house at the shore for the summer. Joining a group house is a great way to expand your social circle; you might not date house members, but you'll meet all their friends. I met the man in my life when we were both members of the same group house (we began dating after we'd been friends for two years). Families often rent a house at the shore or the mountains for a week, or several weeks, and sometimes families share a house for the summer.

THE JERSEY SHORE:

HOTLINES

BEACH WEATHER (609) 646-6400

> **HELPFUL HINTS:** Stand on the beach and look as far as you can, and you'll just see a swarm of people. Walk and you'll notice that there are imperceptible border lines every few blocks. Within a 40 block span you are likely to pass: a singles beach, family beach, volleyball beach, surfing beach, rafting beach, fishing beach, sailing beach (permits required), windsurfers, and an occasional jet ski beach or bay. Sports beaches are pre-designated, and the local Town Hall of the town you want to visit can answer specific questions by phone. (If that doesn't work, try the town police station and ask *them* who to call.) Bays are used by water-skiers, motorized fishing boats, windsurfers and jet skiers.

Vacationers from the Philly area go to beach towns all over the Jersey shore (vacationing New Yorkers mostly go to resorts north of Atlantic City). Atlantic City street parking is metered. All beaches just outside of Atlantic City have a 3 hr street parking limit. Beach areas further away have unrestricted parking. Between Memorial and Labor Day weekends all beach towns (except Atlantic City and Wildwood) require you to buy a "Beach Tag." The income pays for lifeguards, etc. Tags are sold by "Tag Checkers" who sit at beach entrances or wander around the beach. Week tags average $6, Season tags average $12. Few towns sell Day tags. The <u>Philadelphia Inquirer</u> includes a "Shore Guide" in their Memorial Weekend *Friday* edition. It lists contact phone numbers, beach tag prices, what towns have sports beaches, etc., etc.

Families

Families pretty much go anywhere on the Jersey Shore, but the beaches that are true family beaches are the ones with a bathroom and snack shop close by. That's where you'll see lots of kids.

SPECIAL EVENTS/SEASONAL EVENTS   Page 139

Singles

Singles below their early thirties go just about everywhere along the shore. You can usually tell if a night spot is for the very young by the clusters of them standing outside. Wildwood is particularly known for being young and rowdy. The majority of singles, regardless of age, join "group houses" in which several or many members split the expense of a house rental between them. Avalon and Stone Harbor are two major gathering points for singles aged 30 and up. To the North, Long Beach Island has lots of nightlife. Jewish singles hoping to date other Jewish singles often join group houses in the Ventnor/Margate area and enjoy the nightlife in Margate. If you are an older single or couple looking for night life, the best approach is to strike up conversations with couples or singles that look your age. Ask where the good night spots are for your age group. If you want to join a group house next summer, start mentioning this fact to people you meet at social gatherings over the winter. Before long, someone will tell you about a group house. Your other option is to ask various friends and acquaintances if you can visit their group shore house as a weekend guest (expect to pay a "guest fee") or just for the day. This can give you exposure to several different groups, their friends, their hangouts and can be a good way to meet many new people.

Couples

Cape May is particularly quaint and romantic. It has lots of good shops, restaurants, and dozens of Victorian gingerbread style Bed & Breakfasts. Sunset Beach is nearby; you can watch the sunset on the bay.

THE DELAWARE SHORE

REHOBOTH BAY AND DEWEY BEACH IN DELAWARE

Both are loaded with dedicated windsurfers. You will meet weekenders from Pennsylvania, Delaware, Maryland and Washington. Most of the singles crowd consists of groups of people who rent and share large houses for the entire summer. At least one of my male acquaintances swears he's never seen so many attractive women on one beach as at Dewey Beach.

THE POCONOS

HOTLINES

Weather   (610) 337-7777, #2442

HELPFUL HINTS: For obvious reasons, most people tend to gravitate to the areas that are around a lake. There are a few singles on their own, or singles groups that share the cost of a house, but it's not common in the summer. Most of the vacationers are families or couples. You will find lots of swimming, water skiing, fishing, golf, white water rafting, horseback riding, canoeing, kayaking, tennis, bicycling and mountain biking.

Page 140   WINTER HANGOUTS:

OTHER OPTIONS:

FRENCH CREEK STATE PARK   (610) 582-1514

In Elverston, Hopewell Lake allows swimming, and rents rowboats, canoes, sailboats and paddleboats. There are also more than 50 miles of hiking trails.

MARSH CREEK STATE PARK   (610) 458-5119

The lake is great, but you aren't allowed to swim in it. (For that they have a huge supervised swimming pool.) You can rent sailboats, canoes, rowboats, 2 or 3 person paddleboats, or windsurfing equipment (lessons available). I have also seen people with kayaks. Just hanging out on the lovely grass shores of the lake with a picnic is nice. Everybody looks healthy and outdoorsy and it's easy to start up conversations with other singles, families, or couples. Also good for bike rides. Near Downingtown.

| WINTER HANGOUTS: |

LOCAL RESORTS FOR WINTER SPORTS:

| HOTLINES |

Weather   (610) 337-7777, #2442
Road Condition Information   1(800) 847-4872

| HELPFUL HINTS: | Most resorts use manmade snow, very successfully, to maintain slopes from Thanksgiving to around April 1st. Slopes open by 8 am and close by 4 pm; some resorts offer night skiing. By 11 am the slopes are crowded; then they ease up during lunch. Parking is free. Normally, half-day lift tickets are only $5 less than the full day rate. Mid-week and night lift ticket rates are cheaper. Some areas offer a $5 rate for those who only ski between 3 pm and 4 pm. Regulars buy a season ski lift pass for their favorite resort. Discounted lift tickets can be bought through ski clubs, some ski stores, and through Community/Township Recreation Depts. in the Delaware Valley. (Mine offers tickets to Alpine, Jack Frost, Big Boulder, Blue Mountain, Camelback, Doe, Elk, Montage, Shawnee, Spring Mountain and White Tail.) Local Recreation Centers often offer group day trips as well. All resorts offer package-deals for beginners, children and families. Full price lift tickets vary with the resort but are usually in the $25–$35 range. If you are into snowboarding, make sure the resort allows it before you arrive there.

| Singles |

There are a large number of group-rental ski houses in the Poconos. (Some are big, some small, and members might include both singles and couples.) The groups fill yearly vacant spots by networking at ski club meetings, by word of mouth, and occasionally by advertising. The house

SPECIAL EVENTS/SEASONAL EVENTS

renting season starts after Thanksgiving and ends April 1st. Since the snow is not always ideal, many singles go purely for the socializing. Generally, there are more men than women at ski resorts. Since the majority of the singles tend to be in their 20's and early 30's, the older singles usually find one particular nightspot and claim it for their own. To find out where to go, the best thing you can do is approach anyone who looks like they know the area and ask.

Families

Families tend to go to all the resorts. Most ski resorts offer baby-sitting for free, or for a small fee. Sometimes groups of families share the cost of a house together, but most families simply rent a place for one weekend or an entire week.

ALPINE MOUNTAIN at Analomink, PA   (717) 595-2150
Has a 500-ft. vertical drop with 18 trails.

BIG BOULDER at Blakeslee, PA   (717) 722-0100
Offers several nightspots, after-ski Happy Hours at the Blue Heron Lodge, and is very close to Jack Frost and its nightlife. Has night skiing and cross-country trails. Has a 475-ft. vertical drop, 14 trails.

BLUE MARSH at Bernville, PA (near Reading)   (610) 488-6399
A bargain for those on a budget: approx. $16–$24 for full price lift tickets. 300-ft. vertical drop, 11 trails. Has a "Half pipe" for snowboarding.

BLUE MOUNTAIN at Palmerton, PA   (610) 826-7700
Offers night skiing and more. Has a 923-ft. vertical drop, 19 trails.

CAMELBACK at Tannersville, PA   (717) 629-1661
Popular and has lots of singles, but it's crowded. (Skiers also arrive from NY.) Offers night skiing. Has a 800-ft. vertical drop, 25 trails.

DOE MOUNTAIN at Macungie, PA   (610) 682-7109
Offers night skiing. Has a 500-ft. vertical drop, 12 trails. I am told they allow snowboarding.

EAGLE ROCK SKI AREA at Hazelton, PA   (717) 384-6188
Has 12 trails and a 550-ft. vertical drop.

ELK MOUNTAIN at Union Dale, PA   (717) 679-2611
The highest mountain in the area and the most challenging. Offers night skiing. Has a 1,000-ft. vertical drop, 17 trails.

JACK FROST at Blakeslee, PA   (717) 443-8425
Has popular Happy Hours at its lodge and a lot of nearby choices for dancing and nightlife. A lot of singles go there as a result. Also offers cross-country trails (when there is real snow) and special classes and clinics for handicapped skiers. Has a 600-ft. vertical drop, 20 trails.

MONTAGE SKI AREA at Scranton, PA   (717) 969-7669

Gets good reviews from avid skiers. It is a NASTAAR ski area. This means amateurs of all ages and levels can ski on the NASTAAR courses and compare their times against those of the pros. Offers night skiing and special classes for the handicapped. 1,000-ft. vertical drop, 18 trails.

SHAWNEE MOUNTAIN   (717) 421-7231
at Shawnee on Delaware, PA

Also offers night skiing. Has a 700-ft. vertical drop and 23 trails. Allows snowboarding.

SPRING MOUNTAIN at Spring Mountain, PA   (610) 287-7300

A bargain for those on a budget; approx. $14–$17 for full price lift tickets. It's very close to Philadelphia. This is a great mountain for novice skiers. Has a 500-ft. vertical drop, 4 trails. Also offers night skiing.

SOME FUN SEASONAL EVENTS

HELPFUL HINTS: These are a few events that I have found to be really enjoyable, which the public does not always hear a lot about. The exact locations, times, prices, and phone numbers to call will often be listed in Philadelphia Magazine or the Philadelphia Inquirer. I've listed events in monthly sequence. Also, the Friday Philadelphia Inquirer "WEEKEND SECTION" is very helpful. Buy the Friday edition for the two weeks preceding any major holiday (Christmas and New Year's in particular) and you'll find a wealth of information about upcoming festivities to attend.

JANUARY / FEBRUARY / MARCH

AROUND THE WORLD ON WEDNESDAY NIGHTS
at the Philadelphia Museum of Art   (215) 763-8100

Each week has a theme (France, Italy, etc.) with food, tours, a movie, music and socializing opportunities designed accordingly. The event is very popular and many singles turn up, as do the museum regulars. Average age is 30-50. Admission is $6 (food and movie cost extra). A weekly, year-round event. Wednesdays until 8:45 p.m.

BOOKSTORE EVENTS

I believe the whole thing was started by Philadelphia's Borders Bookstore when they built an espresso bar and began offering poetry readings and performances. Then they opened other branches with the same offerings. Now, bookstores like Barnes & Noble, Gene's Books and Encore Books seem to be offering everything from book discussions to ballroom dancing lessons to jazz concerts. For information look through your local paper or check local bookstores.

HIKING CLUB EVENTS

Some hiking clubs offer hikes on major holidays. They are for people who want exercise and companionship. Hiking clubs are listed under Hiking in the Sports category of *Special Interest Organizations*.

SPECIAL EVENTS/SEASONAL EVENTS

MANAYUNK "SECOND SUNDAY" (215) 482-9565.
On the 2nd Sunday of every month, Main Street comes alive with jazz, gallery openings, special store events, wine & cheese and various festival themes. Simply show up, or call the Manayunk Development Corporation for information. Parking can be tough so either go by train or ask if they are running "Park and Ride" shuttle buses.

SPORTS AFTER DARK
No, not the kind that you watch! Most of us know that tennis is often played at night. Several local resorts offer night skiing (see Index). Batona Hiking Club offers Friday Night Moonlight Hikes (see Index). Limerick Golf Course offers night golf from May to Mid-October. They fit individuals and groups into evening tournaments. For $25 you get a glow-in-the-dark ball, golf-cart, beer and snacks. After the game, you can party and dance in their on-site clubhouse/nightclub. (610) 495-6945

OLD CITY ARTS DISTRICT "FIRST FRIDAY" (215) 636-1666.
On the 1st Friday of every month *(except July, August, September)*, almost 40 art and antique galleries in 3 blocks of Philadelphia's Olde City remain open until 8:30 p.m. Many serve wine with munchies. Either simply turn up, or call the Philadelphia Visitor Center for information.

PHILADELPHIA "MAKE IT A NIGHT" (215) 636-1666
Designed to encourage night life in Center City every Wednesday night. Shops stay open later, sidewalk activities are encouraged, and parking is free after 5:00 pm on most streets. (High traffic streets are free after 6:30 pm and some parking lots only charge $1.)

PENNSYLVANIA WINERIES
There are almost 40 of them, some among the oldest in the country. Many are close by and welcome visitors. One of the best known is Chadds Ford Winery, which has wine tasting classes and holiday related events in Chadds Ford (610) 388-6221. Try calling your County Tourist Bureau to track down other Wineries. (I have listed Tourist Bureaus under the New Residents section of *Local Supportive Organizations*.)

PHILADELPHIA RESTAURANT SCHOOL (215) 222-4200
They have a restaurant and a pastry shop as well. Give it a try one of these days. Call to find out more and make reservations.

THE RADNOR HOTEL (610) 688-5800
If you don't mind live music and cigarette smoke, if you feel comfortable in a Main Line crowd and are in the 30–50's age range, this is the place for you. Wednesdays through Fridays are the best evenings for singles. Don't get into a rut and get hooked into a weekly ritual—just try it every now and then. The Hotel is on Lancaster Avenue in St. Davids.

THE ACADEMY BALL (215) 893-1935
"One of the major events in Philadelphia Society," now approx. in its 135th year. The full program consists of a performance at the Academy of Music, with a supper and ball afterwards (in 3 different nearby locations). Held in mid-to-late January. Call for information.

SOME FUN SEASONAL EVENTS

PHILADELPHIA FLOWER SHOW (215) 625-8250

Held in the beginning of March; it's a welcome reminder that Spring is just around the corner. The displays are quite amazing. As of 1996, it will be held in the Philly Convention Center. Call for information.

THE BOOK AND THE COOK

An annual four-day event featuring noted chefs and cookbook authors, who give demonstrations and then serve fixed-price dinners at area restaurants. Thousands of people sign up for this orgy of gourmet eating. Special events for adults and children. Held in mid-March. Call the Philadelphia Visitor's Center for information (215) 636-1666.

APRIL / MAY / JUNE

ANNUAL RITES OF SPRING (215) 238-3970

An off-shoot of the autumn Goose Ball, this party kicks off the spring season and features munchies, drinks, and dancing to a D.J. Attracts a large stylish singles crowd. Held at the end of April. For information, or to be on the mailing list, call the Deborah Hospital Foundation.

VALBORGSMASSOAFTON (215) 389-1776

A Swedish festival to welcome the arrival of spring with a bonfire, singing, dancing and refreshments, at the Swedish Museum. End of April.

PHILADELPHIA KITE FESTIVAL (215) 685-0052

A professional event featuring red, white and blue kites in Fairmount Park. End of April. Call Fairmount Park Events information or check newspapers for details.

POINT TO POINT AT WINTERTHUR (302) 888-4600

In early May, near Wilmington. Annual event featuring antique cars, equestrian events, a carriage parade, music, and tailgate picnic contest.

MAY DAY CELEBRATION WITH THE PHILADELPHIA REVELS

The Philadelphia Revels celebrate May Day with a May pole dance outside the Suburban Square shopping center in Ardmore. Other festivities are offered as well. Call the Philadelphia Revels at (610) 688-5303.

DADVAIL REGATTA

The pinnacle race of the rowing season. Rowing crews arrive days ahead, and both shores of the Schuylkill (Kelly Drive and West River Drive) are covered with boats. Both roads are closed to traffic. The events are fun to watch. Mid-May. (Check newspapers for details.)

THE DEVON HORSE SHOW (610) 964-0550

Begins the Friday before Memorial weekend and lasts one week. There are riding and jumping competitions, marching bands, fun events with dogs, shopping booths and amusement park rides. You pay admission to get into the grounds and can stand or walk around as you watch the events. In Devon, on the Main Line. Call for information.

SPECIAL EVENTS/SEASONAL EVENTS

FESTIVAL OF FOUNTAINS (610) 388-6741

Illuminated fountain displays occur every evening at Longwood Gardens. Occasionally the displays follow a concert, and on other days they are accompanied by fireworks. (Tickets must be purchased in advance for fireworks nights and for <u>some</u> of the concert nights.) *June through September.*

THE MANN MUSIC CENTER

Located in Fairmount Park. The amphitheater is partially covered, partially open-air and the rearmost portion of the seating consists of a grassy lawn which is perfect for picnics. Every year, groups of friends, dates and families sit on blankets and have picnics while they enjoy the music. *Between June and August, the midweek concerts are by The Philadelphia Orchestra, and free tickets for the grassy lawn (picnic) area can be obtained* by mailing in coupons found in the Philadelphia Inquirer (Wed., Thurs. and Sunday editions). Park on the street near the Center, or follow the signs for organized paid parking beside the Center. Concerts of other types are also given throughout the summer, but none of those tickets are free; instead, the cheapest tickets are for the lawn area.

RADNOR HUNT STEEPLECHASE RACES (610) 388-2700

Held on the 3rd Saturday in May; observers bring their families and dogs, picnics and friends. Everyone watches the horses before they head off and tries to guess who'll win. A carriage parade and display of vintage cars are also offered. The races are held in Malvern on country grounds behind a clubhouse. For information call the Brandywine Conservancy.

ZOOBILEE (215) 243-1100

Annual fund-raiser party for the Philadelphia Zoo which attracts lots of stylish singles. Food, entertainment and a live band for dancing usually make things fun. Held in early June.

JULY / AUGUST / SEPTEMBER

PICK YOUR OWN FRUIT (610) 876-8796 (Hotline)

Linvilla Orchards, in Media. They offer "Pick your own peaches" starting in July and "Pick your own apples" a little bit later. I'm not even sure what else they offer, so call and ask. The fruit picking season usually lasts until late September. They have a daily status hot line.

"NIGHT IN VENICE" BOAT PARADE AND BAY CELEBRATION

Held in early July in Ocean City, NJ. This is one event you need to plan for <u>way</u> ahead of time. Boats entered in the parade are decorated with a theme and lights; homes around the bays are also decorated. The whole thing happens in the early evening, but traffic is blocked from entering the island by mid-day. The catch is, you must either know someone who owns a home on the bay, know someone who owns a boat (so you can watch the parade from the water), or book ahead of time to be on one of the group rental boats that sits just outside the bays. Very few observation locations are public. For information call (609) 399-6111 ext. 222.

SOME FUN SEASONAL EVENTS

BASTILLE DAY ANNIVERSARY (215) 735-5283
Every July 14th the Alliance Francaise has a big party in some Center City location with music, dance, etc.

PORT INDIAN REGATTA AND HYDROPLANE RACES
Eight classes of American Powerboat-sanctioned races and a water skiing exhibition. Mid-July. Check newspapers for details.

SUMMER BEACH EVENTS
Most beach towns offer summer events. Event schedules are in brochure form and are found in local shops. Look for Sand Sculpture contests. The one in Avalon, NJ is in early August, and the sculptures are wonderful—entire families and groups of friends make them. I also love the annual life guard races; it's "Bay Watch" in real life. Ask your local beach lifeguards where and when the races are being held.

THE SNOBALL (609) 931-4462
The Fall Line Ski Club kicks off the social season with a big party and dance in Cherry Hill. It's not formal and there is no snow; it's really just an excuse to socialize and mingle. Partygoers' average age range is 20's through 40's, and they are mostly single. Early September.

FUND RAISING GROUPS
The National Kidney Foundation, and similar organizations, raise funds by sponsoring parties, dances and events. The season starts in autumn. **They always attract a large number of upscale singles, many in the 30–50 age range.** Other non-profit groups are listed in the Disease/Injury Related category under *Local Supportive Organizations*. Ask them about events they offer.

OCTOBER / NOVEMBER / DECEMBER

APPLE FESTIVAL (215) 794-4000
In early November, Peddler's Village in Lahaska (Bucks County) features crafts-people from all over the country, along with foods made from apples (apple butter, cider, fritters, pie, etc.). Peddler's Village is a picturesque collection of shops. After mid-November the Village features Christmas lights, candle luminaries, and an incredibly elaborate gingerbread house competition.

THE RADNOR HUNT FALL 3-DAY EVENT (610) 644-9918
Held in the middle of October, on land behind a clubhouse in Radnor. Observers bring picnics, friends, families and dogs. Top steeplechase horses and riders compete in various events. Once, I was at a picnic alongside the cross-country route; we talked and played guitar while one person did "scout duty," signaling for quiet whenever a horse and rider approached. For information call The Radnor Hunt.

THE MARSHALTON TRIATHLON
This is a triathlon your grandmother could finish. You bike 2 1/2 miles (downhill), canoe 2 1/2 miles (badly and often backwards), walk back 2 1/2 miles (no running allowed) and bike 2 1/2 miles (often walking

your bike uphill). Most entrants simply have a good time and enjoy all the partying that goes on before, during and after the event. Last time I entered there were 1,700 people in the race with many more watching. To enter, call the Marshalton Inn (near West Chester) after Labor Day (610) 692-4367. If you have problems, try the Marshalton Fire Dept. (It's a fund raiser for them.) It's held the 1st Sunday in October. By the way, they can help you find a partner for the canoe portion—you do need one.

THE GOOSE BALL   (215) 238-3970

There are no geese and it's not a formal ball, but it is held the first week of October (annually) and it's always jammed. The Philadelphia location varies, but most of the sophisticated, single professionals (20's–40's) in the area attend it and have a good time dancing to a DJ or live music. For information call the Deborah Hospital Foundation.

THE BEAUX ARTS BALL   (215) 569-3187

This ball always has a theme, and the many people who attend it (20's–40's) wear black-tie or creative costumes (often as a group—many are architects or designers). This is an experience you should try at least once. There are never less than 4 dance bands. Location varies but the time is Halloween. The Foundation for Architecture has details.

IKEA'S CHRISTMAS TREE LEASING

Each year, before Christmas, Ikea "Leases" Christmas trees for $20. After Christmas you return the tree to Ikea; they put it through a grinder to make mulching and you get $10. The con's are that the trees dry out fairly quickly. The pro's are that it's ideal for someone on a budget; it's a great way to feel less guilty about cutting down a tree; and hauling your tree back isn't as bad as it sounds (most people wrap it in an old bedsheet). The fragrance of pine needles that surrounds the parking lot is SO ABSOLUTELY MESMERIZING that you'll probably decide to hang out by the mulcher for awhile and watch other people drag their trees out of their cars. At Plymouth Meeting Mall, mid-December.

CHESTNUT HILL STAG AND DOE NIGHTS

In December, every Wednesday before Christmas, the shops at Chestnut Hill (which are already picturesque) stay open until 9 pm. Lit candles and decorations are everywhere. Mulled cider and munchies are provided to prospective shoppers wandering from one shop to the next.

ILLUMINAIRE NITES IN SKIPPACK VILLAGE

On Wednesday nights in December, the shops and walkways in Skippack village are decorated with candles. They usually also serve mulled cider with munchies. It's really a pretty sight to behold.

THE CHRISTMAS REVELS   (610) 688-5303

The Philadelphia Revels celebrate both the shortest day of the year and Christmas by performing at Swarthmore College in mid-December. Wearing garb from the ancient days of England and Europe, the performers do "olde worlde" songs, dances, skits, Christmas carol sing-a-longs, and even manage to convince the audience to link hands with them and skip around the theatre. Call the Philadelphia Revels.

SOME FUN SEASONAL EVENTS

LUCIA FEST
Swedish Historical Museum   (215) 389-1776
Olde Swedes Church   (215) 389-1513

Early December. A traditional Swedish Christmas with girls wearing wreaths of candles on their heads and Swedish food and crafts. At the Olde Swedes Church and at the American Swedish Historical Museum.

CHESTER COUNTY GROWN   (610) 344-6285
Chester Cnty. Agriculture Devel. Council
West Chester, PA

This is a booklet with a detailed list of Christmas tree farms in Chester County that offer live Christmas trees for replanting or cutting down (by you). The booklet is free; just contact the council. The rest is up to you.

WASHINGTON CROSSING THE DELAWARE   (609) 737-0623
Titusville, NJ

On Christmas Day there is a reenactment of General Washington's crossing the Delaware. I am told that it is both interesting and fun. Both the PA and NJ sides of the river have many festive, holiday things going on on at the time of the event.

THINGS TO DO ON NEW YEAR'S EVE

Buy the Philadelphia Inquirer on the Friday before New Year's Eve. There will be a listing of typical parties at bars and restaurants for which you can try to make a reservation, but there will also be a listing of more unusual activities. You might discover that you could attend a concert, spend the night Swing Dancing with the Swing Dance Society or go in costume to an operatic listen-and-sing-along with the Delaware Valley Opera Company. I once did the latter with a date. He kept saying "This is the weirdest New Year's Eve I have ever spent—but this is fun!!!"

NEW YEAR'S EVE AND NEW YEAR'S DAY PARTICIPATORY RACES

This is something you would need to locate in December. Look for brochures in athletic and running shoe stores around you. Some races are on New Year's Eve, others on New Year's Day; some promote locally and others promote on a larger scale. They often encourage theme costumes; you'll see lots of people wearing diapers! I ran in a 5K race on New Year's Day of 1989 (along Kelly Drive) and it was the best way I have ever started a year off. I highly recommend it! By the way, watch out for those paper water cups; sometimes they contain champagne!

INDEX

A

A.A.R.P., 117
About Dating Services, 134
Abraxas Foundation, 42
The Academy Ball, 143
Academy Of Model Aeronautics, 27
Access to the World: travel guide, 103
Action Alliance for Parents of the Deaf, 102
Action Alliance of Senior Citizens, 117
Addiction Help Line, 82
Addiction Info.& Referral Line, 82
Adoption Forum, 94
Adult & Family Services, 85
Adult Children of Alcohol. & Dysfunc. , 83
Advertising Communication Times, 123
Afro-American Museum, 76
Afro-American Quilters (Quilters of Round), 26
Afro-American Ski Club (Blazers), 69
Agencies for the Aging, 115, 119
AIDS Hotline (National), 86, 107
AIDS Hotline (Philadelphia), 86, 107
AIDS Information Network, 87
Airplane Model Flyers, 27
Al-Anon Family Groups Del. Valley, 83
Al-Assist, 83
Alateen, 83
Alcohol Addiction, 83
Alcohol Hotline (addiction), 82
Alcohol. & Addict. Council of Del. Co., 83
Alcoholics Anonymous, 83
All Addictions, 85
Allen's Lane Theater, 35
Alliance for the Mentally Ill of E. PA, 88
Alliance Francaise of Philadelphia, 76
Alphorn Ski Association, 70
Alpine Mountain, 141
ALS Association, 87
Alzheimer's Disease, 87
Amateur Chamber Music Players, 23
Ambler Choral Society, 38
Ambler Symphony, 39
Amer. Assoc. of Retired Persons, 117
America-Italy Society, 76
American Anorexia/Bulimia Assoc., 85
American Assoc. of Individual Investors, 8
American Association of Suicidology, 90
American Business Women's Assoc., 11
American Cancer Society, 87
American Diabetes Association, 87
American Heart Association, 31, 88
American Institute of Wine & Food, 30
American Kidney Foundation, 88
American Liver Foundation, 88
American Lung Association, 88
American Parkinson Disease Assoc., 88
American Radio Relay League, 28
American Red Cross, 31
American Sewing Guild, 26
American Youth Hostel Sailing Club, 67
Ample Awakenings, 45
Amtrak Customer Relations, 103
Andalusia Community Theater Co., 35
Anna Crusis Choir, 38
Annual Rites of Spring Party, 144
Appalachian Mountain Club, 55
Apple Festival at Peddler's Village, 146
Architecture, 14
Around the World on Wed. Nights, 142
Art, 15
Art Directors Club, 8
Art Lovers Exchange, 45
Art Matters Newspaper, 123
Arthritis Foundation, 87
Artists Theater Association, 35
Assoc. for Speech & Hearing Hotline, 86
Assoc. of PC Professionals, 13
Associated Services for the Blind, 102
Asthma & Allergy Foundation, 87
Astrology, 27
Astronomy, 27
Audubon Community Orchestra, 39
Audubon Society, 40
Autistic Children (National Assoc. for), 87

B

B'nai B'rith Singles Unit, 45
Bachelors Barge Club, 65
Bala-Cynwyd Symphony, 39
The Barnstormers, 35
Basecamp, 64
Bastille Day Anniversary , 146
Batona Hiking Club, 61, 143
The Beaux Arts Ball, 147
Beth El Jewish Singles, 45

INDEX

Bicycle Club of Philadelphia, 56
Bicycle Coalition of the Delaware Valley, 56
Bicycling, 56
Bicycling Federation of Pennsylvania, 56
Big Apple Dinner Theater, 35
Big Boulder, 141
Big Brother-Big Sister, 94
The Birth Center, 95
Birth Oriented Resource Network, 95
Blackwell Birth Center for Women, 88
Blackwell Health Center for Women, 107
Blazers Ski Club, 69
Blue Marsh, 141
Blue Mountain, 141
Boardsailing, 74
The Book and the Cook, 144
Bookstore Events, 21, 142
Boy Scouts, 31
Brandywine Bicycle Club, 56
Brandywine Conservancy, 40
Brandywine River Museum, 22
Brandywine Road Runners Club, 66
Brandywine Valley Ski Association, 70
The Brandywiners, 35
The Bridge Players, 35
Buck Ridge Ski Club, 70
Bucks County Choral Society, 37
Bucks County Legal Aid, 104
Bucks County Singers, 38
Bucks County Ski Club, 70
Bucks County Symphony, 39
Bucks County Tourist Commission, 112
Bucks County White Tail Disc Golf Club, 59
Bucks Mount Ski Club, 71
Bucks-Mont Astronomical Assoc., 27
Bureau of Small Business Devel., 106
Bureau of Women's Business Devel., 106
The Burlington County Footlighters, 35
Burn Survivors, 87
Business and Prof. Women's Club, 11
Business Groups for Women, 11
Business Philadelphia Newspaper, 123
Bux-Mont Mac User Group, 13
Buxmont Computer User Group, 13

C

C.A.R.I.E., 117
C.D.C National STD (support), 89
C.O.R.A. (counsel. & Ref. Assist.), 85
Cafe Israel Folk Dancing, 17 - 18
Cajun Dancing, 19

Camelback, 141
Cancer, 87
Cancer Information Hotline, 86
Cancer Information Service, 87
Canoeing, 58
Cape May, 139
Career and Counseling Center, 113
Caregiver Support Groups, 95
Catholic Alumni Club of Philadelphia, 45
Catholic Family Life Bureau, South Jersey, 85, 89, 91, 95, 108, 115, 118
Catholic Social Services, Philadelphia, 85, 89, 91, 95, 108, 115, 118
Centennial Singers, 38
Center City Home Schoolers, 95
Center Philharmonic, 39
Central Bucks Bicycle Club, 56
Cerebral Palsy Assoc., 87
Chamber of Commerce, 8
Chapel St. Players, 35
Cheltenham People's Theater, 35
Chess, 28
Chester Co. Grown Christmas Trees, 148
Chester County Band, 39
Chester County Tourist Bureau, 112
Chester County Trail Club, 62
Chestnut Hill Stag and Doe Nights, 147
Chestnut Hill Symphony, 39
Child and Parent Center, 95
Children (Kids), 31
Children of Aging Parents, Inc., 95
Choral Arts Society of Philadelphia, 37
Choral Society of Montgomery County, 37
The Christian Support Guide, 49
Christian Church Groups, 95
Christian Powersource, 46
Christian Support Guide, 95
Church Support Groups, 90
City Paper, 123
Classical Music (Participatory), 23
Club Sashay, 20
Co-Dependants Anonymous, 85
Cobbs Creek Golf Course, 59 - 60
Cocaine Hotline (Phoenix House), 83
Collectors, 30
Colonial Playhouse, 35
Community Accountants, 77, 106
Community Legal Services, 104
Community Service Clubs, 34
Community Singles, 46
Compassionate Friends, Inc., 90

INDEX

Connecting in Philadelphia (a book), 129
Connections, 46
Connelly Center, 22
Contact Philadelphia, Inc., 77, 89, 118
    Hotline, 82, 90, 94, 107, 117
Contraceptive Advice Hotline, 107
Counseling & Crisis Hotline, 107
Counseling Net. for Loss & Transition, 91
The Couple Gourmet, 30
CPR Lessons, 31
Crafts (Handicrafts), 26
Crescent Boat Club, 65
Crime Victim Center, 108
Crisis Intervention for Mental Health Hotline, 82
Crohn's & Colitis Foundation, 87
Cue & Curtain Players, 35
Cycles Bikyle & Scott-Bikyle Flyers, 57

D

Dadvail Regatta, 144
Daemion House Adolescents' Crisis Hotline, 82, 94
Dance! Magazine, 20
Dance
    Non-Participatory, 24
    Participatory, 15
Dancing:
    All Types, 15
    Ballroom/Social Dance, 15
    Country Western, 16
    Folk, 16
    Square, 20
    Swing Dance, 20
Debtors Anonymous, 84
Del-Ches User Group, 13
Del. Val. Fed. of Sq. & Round Dancers, 20
Del. Valley Amateur Astronomers, 27
Del. Valley American Youth Hostels, 57, 62
Del. Valley Hobby Greenhouse Assoc., 41
Delaware Cnty Women Against Rape, 107
Delaware County Legal Aid, 104
Delaware County Magazine, 123
Delaware County Road Runners, 66
Delaware County Symphony, 39
Delaware County Tourist Bureau, 112
Delaware Today Magazine, 124
Delaware Underwater Swim Club, 72
Delaware Valley Bicycle Club, 57
Delaware Valley Boardsailing Assoc., 74
Delaware Valley Choral Society, 24, 38

Delaware Valley Computer User, 124
Delaware Valley Folk Music Alliance, 23
Delaware Valley Opera Company, 24, 36
Delaware Valley Orienteering Assoc., 63
Democratic Party, 43
Depts. of Recreation/Depts. of Parks, 31, 54
The Devon Horse Show, 144
Dewey Beach, 139
Diabetes, 87
Dial an Expert (a book), 130
Diamond State Bicycle Club, 57
Disc Golf, 59
Diversified Investor Group, 8
Doc's Divers Dive Club, 72
Doctor's Orchestra, 39
Doe Mountain, 141
The Drama Group, 35
Drama Ink, 35
The Dramateurs, 35
Drexel Hill Players, 35
Drexel Univ. College of Business, 105
Drug Addiction, 83
Dutch Country Players, 35
Dynamic Diversions, 55
Dyslexia, 103

E

Eagle Rock Ski Area, 141
Eastern Amputee Golf Assoc., 75
Eastern Pennsylvania Ski Council, 68
Eastern Surfing Association, 72
Ed 'Porky' Oliver Golf Club, 59 - 60
Education Info. & Resource Center, 101
Elk Mountain, 141
Embroiderers Guild of America., 26
Energy for Employment, 113
Entrepreneur's Club of the Del. Valley, 9
Entry by Audition and Invitation:
    Choral, 37
    Instrumental, 39
    Theatrical, 35
Episcopal Community Service, Phila. area, 85, 89, 91, 96, 108, 115, 118
Epsilon New, 46
Ethical Culture Society, 32
Exchange Club, 34
Executive Women's Golf League, 61

INDEX

F

Fairmount Rowing Association, 65
Fall Line Ski Club, 71
Families Anonymous, 85
Families of Murder Victims, Inc., 91
Family & Social Serv. of Delaware County, 85, 89, 91, 96, 108, 115, 118
Family Connections, 96
Family Forum, 96
Family Friends, 78
Family Learning Center, 96
Family Service of Bucks County, 85, 89, 91, 96, 108, 115, 118
Family Service of Chester County, 85, 89, 91, 96, 108, 115, 118
Family Service of Montgomery County, 85, 89, 91, 96, 108, 115, 118
Family Service of Philadelphia County, 85, 89, 91, 96, 108, 115, 118
Fan Clubs / Enthusiast Clubs, 28
Fast Tracks, 66
Fathers & Children Equality, 97
Fathers & Children Together, 97
Fathers' Right Hotline, 94
Fellowship of Catholic Adults, 46
Fencing, 58
Festival of Fountains, 145
Fifty Hikes in Eastern Pennsylvania (a book), 129
50 Plusers, 46
Film Forum, 22
Filmbill Rendezvous, 22, 46
Fine Art/Folk Art, 15
First Call for Help, 97
First Call for Help Hotline, 82, 86, 90, 94, 107, 117
Fishing, 28
The Fitness Network, 55
Flying Solo, 108
Folk Dance, 16
Folk Dance Council of the Del. Valley, 17
Folk Dancing, 19
Folk Dancing:
   American, English and Scottish Country, 17
   Cajun, 19
   Contra, 18 - 19
   English Country, 17 - 18
   International, 17 - 19
   International Folk & Western Squares, 18
   Irish, 19
   Israeli, 17 - 19
   Scottish Country, 19
Folk Music (Participatory), 23
Food & Beverage Appreciation Groups, 30
Food Addiction (Weight Related), 84
Footlighters Theater, 36
Foreign Policy Research Inst., 43
Forge Theater Company, 35
Forty Plus of Philadelphia, 113
Foster Grandparent Program, 78
Foundation for Architecture, 14
Franklin D. Roosevelt Golf Course, 60
Franklin Institute, 22
Freewheelers, 47
French Creek State Park, 140
Fresh-Start Divorce Support Groups, 91
Friendly Singles 50 Plus, 47
Friends of Philadelphia Parks, 41
Friends of the Phila. Museum of Art, 23
Frisbee, 59
Frisbee Golf, 59
Fund Raising Group Parties, 146

G

Gales Encyclopedia of Associations, 130
Gam-Anon Family Services, 84
Gamblers Anonymous, 84
Gambling Addiction, 84
Garden State Chorale, 38
Garden State Discovery Museum, 47
Gatherings of Business Women, 12
Gay & Lesbian Community Center, 109
Gay & Lesbian Switchboard, 108
Gay Support Organizations, 107 - 108
Gay Violence (anti-gay) Hotline, 107
General Wayne Inn, 15
Geographical Society of Philadelphia, 76
German Society of Pennsylvania, 76
Germantown Country Dancers, 17
Gershman YM & YWHA, 16, 47
Getting the Love You Want (a book), 131
Gilbert & Sullivan Soc. of Ches. County, 35
Girl Scouts, 32
Gloria Dei Singles, 47
Golden Eagle Community Band, 39
The Golden Times, 124
Golf
   Ladies' Public Course Golf Leagues, 60
   Men's Public Course Leagues, 59
The Goose Ball, 147
Gratz Jewish Community College, 39

INDEX

Great Books Discussion Groups, 21
Great Valley Career Connections, 113
The Greater Philadelphia Job Bank Book, 113, 129
Greater Phila. Cultural Alliance, 112 - 113
Greater Phila. Senior Citizen Resource Dir., 124
Greeter-Newcomers of Newtown Sq., 111
Guide to Jewish Philadelphia, 129

H

H.E.R.S. Foundation (hysterectomy), 88
H.U.G.S., 47
Haddonfield Plays & Players, 35
Haddonfield Singles Ministry, 47
Haddonfield Symphony, 39
Ham Radio, 28
Handicapped:
   Sports, 75
Handicrafts, 26
The Hash House Harriers, 66
Haverford College Symphony, 39
Heart Related (disease), 88
Helping Other People Evolve, 91
Hemophilia Foundation of Del. Valley, 88
Heritage, 76
Herpes Social Solutions, 47
Hiking, 61
Hobbies, 27
Homeopathy, 31
Homicide Support Groups, 91
Horse-Shoe Trail Club, 62
Horseback Riding, 63
Hosea, 47
Hospital Support Groups, 89, 91
Hotlines:
   Addiction Related Category, 82
   Beach Weather, 138
   Children Category, 94
   Cocaine Hotline (Phoenix House), 83
   Consumer Protection, 122
   Disease or Injury Related Category, 86
   Divorced Category, 90
   Family Group Category, 94
   Family Individuals Category, 94
   Federal Information Center, 122
   Gay Support Organizations, 107
   Governor's Action Center, 122
   Handicapped/Disabled Category, 101
   In Mourning Category, 90
   Mayor's Action Center, 122
   Men's and Women's Issues Category, 107
   New Residents Category, 110
   Philadelphia Weather, 122
   Poconos Weather, 139
   Recycling, 122
   Recycling in Bucks County, 122
   Recycling in Chester County, 122
   Recycling in Delaware County, 122
   Recycling in Montgomery County, 122
   Recycling in Philadelphia, 122
   Recycling, PA Resources Council, 122
   Separated Category, 90
   Stamps by phone, 122
   Suicide & Crisis Intervention Services, 83
   Time, 122
   Widowed Category, 90
   Youth Crisis Line, 83
   Zipcode Information, 122
How to visit New York cheaply, 122
How to Work the Competition (a book), 131
Huntingdon Valley Ski Club, 71
Hysterectomy, 88

I

Ikea's Christmas Tree Leasing, 147
Illuminaire Nites in Skippack Village, 147
Immaculata College Orchestra, 39
Incest Survivors Anonymous, 97
Interfaith Working Group, 108
International Cinema, 22
International Folk Dancing, 18
International House of Philadelphia, 76
International Wine Club, 30
Introductory Organizations, 111

J

J.A.S.S. Hotline, 47
Jack Frost, 141
Jaycees, 9
Jewish Assoc. of Singles Services, 47
Jewish Business Network, 9
Jewish Community Centers:, 32, 54, 119
   Kaiserman Branch, 48
   Klein Branch, 48
   Southern New Jersey, 35, 48
   Wilmington Branch, 48
Jewish Family & Children's Serv., Phila. area, 85, 89, 91, 97, 108, 115, 118
Jewish Family & Children's Serv., Southern NJ, 85, 89, 91, 108, 115, 118
Jewish Family Services (NJ), 108

INDEX

Jewish Prof. & Business Singles, 48
Jewish Single Parent Network, 48
The Job Seekers Guide to the Delaware Valley, 113
The Job Seeker's Guide to the Delaware Valley, 129
Job-Search Support Group, 114
John F. Byrne Golf Course, 60
Jugglers Club, 29
Juggling, 29
Juniata Golf Course, 60
The Junior League, 33
Juvenile Diabetes Foundation, 87

K

K. P. Corral, 16
Kennett Symphony, 39
Keystone Diving Association, 72
Kidney Disease, 88
Kids, 31
The King of Prussia Players, 36
King of Prussia Ski Club, 69
King Squares Dance Club, 20
Kite Flying, 29
Kiwanis International, 34

L

La Leche League, 97
Labyrinth Newspaper, 124
Lambertville Country Dancers, 18
Landskater In-line Skate Club, 64
Langhorne Players, 36
Language, 76
Lansdowne Symphony, 39
LaSalle Univ., Sm. Business Devel. Ctr., 105
Lawyer Referral Services, 104
Le TIP, 9
Leadership Inc., 77
Leads Club, 9
League of Women Voters, 43
Learning Disabilites Assoc. of PA, 97
Legal Aid of Chester County, 104
Legal Hotline for Older Americans, 104
Legal Services for Various Counties, 104
Lesbian Support Organizations, 107 - 108
Leukemia Society of America, 88
Liberty Bell Wanderers, 62
Liberty Yacht Club, 67
Library for the Blind & Physically Disab., 101

Limerick Golf Course, 143
Lions Club, 34
Literacy Council, 77
Literature, 21
Little League, 31
Little League Challenger Division, 75
Live and Learn, 114
The Lively Arts Group, 24
Liver Disease, 88
Local Sports Bar Leagues, 32, 54
Long Distance Love, 89, 102
Lower Bucks Computer User Group, 13
Lower Merion-Narberth Coalition, 118
Lucia Fest at Christmas, 148
Lung Disease, 88
Lupus Foundation of Philadelphia, 88
Lutheran Children & Family Serv. of E. PA, 85, 89, 91, 97, 108, 115, 118
Lutheran Settlement House, 114

M

Macintosh Business Users Society, 13
Macuser Group of Delaware, 13
Macuser Group of S. New Jersey, 13
Magee Rehabilitation Hospital, 75, 101
Magicians, 29
Main Line Community Big Band, 39
Main Line Macintosh User Group, 13
Main Line Magazine, 124
Main Line School Night Association, 124
Main Line Ski Club, 69
Main Line Symphony, 39
Mainly Bikes, 57
Malta Boat Club, 65
Management in Transition, 114
Manayunk Second Sunday, 143
The Mann Music Center, 145
Mantalk, 109
Marple Newtown Players, 36
Marple-Newtown String Ensemble, 39
Marsh Creek State Park, 140
The Marshalton Triathlon, 146
The Masterworks Chorale, 38
Matchmaking Services (description of), 135
Mate-Search International, Databank, 48
Matthew Lesko Books, 130
Mayor's Commission for Women, 107
Mayor's Commission on Aging Hotline, 117
Mayor's Office for the Handicapped, 101
Medicare Hotline, 86
The Men's Resource Center, 92, 109, 114

INDEX

Mendelssohn Club of Philadelphia, 38
Mensa, 33
Mental Illness, 88
Merion Musical Band, 39
Merion Musical Society, 39
Methacton Community Theater, 36
MetroKids Magazine, 124
Middle Atlantic Road Runners Club, 66
Middletown Country Club, 60
Mixed Doubles for Singles, 53
Moms Club, 97
Montage Ski Area, 142
Montgomery County Legal Aid, 104
Montgomery County Visitors Bureau, 112
Montgomery Theater, 36
Montgomery Women's Network, 12
More to Love, 48
Mosaic Outdoor Mountain Club, 55
Moss Rehabilitation Hospital, 75, 101
Mothers Against Drunk Driving, 92
Mothers of Twins Club, 98
Mothers Without Custody, 98
Mothers' Associations, 98
Movies/Cinema, 22
MPC Singles 21+, 48
Music
   Non-participatory, 24
   Participatory, 23, 37, 39

N

N.A.A.F.A., 48, 108
Nar-Anon, 83
Narberth Community Players, 36
Narcotic Addiction, 83
Narcotics Anonymous, 83
Nat'l Alliance for the Mentally Ill Hotline, 86
Nat'l Assoc. of Female Executives, 12
Nat'l Assoc. of Women Business Owners, 12
Nat'l Assoc. to Advance Fat Acceptance, 48, 108
Nat'l Health Information Ctr. Hotline, 86
National Alliance for the Mentally Ill, 107
National Brotherhood of Skiers, 69
National Center for Homeopathy, 31
National Center for Stuttering, 102
National Council on Aging Hotline, 86, 117
National Council on Alcoholism, 84
National Down Syndrome Congress, 102
National Down Syndrome Society, 102
National Fantasy Fan Club, 28

National Inst. on Drug Abuse Hotline, 83
National Org. for Women, 43, 92, 109
National Self-Help Clearing House, 85, 90, 98, 102, 108, 118
National Stuttering Project, 103
National VD Hotline, 86
Nature Walks for Adult Singles, 48
Neighborhood Parenting Programs, 98
Nervous/Emotional Illness, 88
Neshaminy Valley Music Theater, 36
Network of the Church of the Savior, 49
Network of Victim Assistance, 108
Networking Professionals, 9
New Beginnings, 92
New Choices, Bucks Cnty. C.C., 114
New Choices, Delaware Cnty. C.C, 114
New Choices, Montgomery Cnty. C.C, 114
New Hope Nordics, 69
New Jersey Monthly Magazine, 125
New Jersey Poetry Society, 21
New Year's Races, 148
Newcomers Club of Bryn Mawr, 111
Newcomers Club of Great Valley, 112
Newcomers Groups, 111
Newspaper Listings for Bereavement Groups, 92
Newspapers for Older Adults, 118
Nicotine Anonymous, 84
"Night In Venice" Celebration, 145
Night Golf, 143
Night Skiing, 141, 143
NJ/PA Songwriters Association, 23
Norristown Chorale, 39
North Penn Ski Club, 69
North Penn Symphony, 39
Northeast Jewish Community Singles, 49
Northeast Road Runners Club, 66
Northeast Singles Club, 49
Nursing Mothers (Mothers' Assoc.), 98
Nursing Mothers' Advisory Council, 98

O

Obsessive Compulsive Foundation, 86
Old City Arts District First Friday, 143
Old York Road Symphony, 39
Older Adults Guide for Services in Mont. Co., 125
Older Pennsylvanians Handbook A Guide..., 125
Olyney Symphony, 39
Omni Speed Club, 64

INDEX

On the Air Magazine, 125
Open Land Conservancy, 41
Opera (Non-participatory), 24
Opera Appreciation Club, 25
The Opera Club, 25
Options Career and Human Resource, 114
Orchestra Society, 40
Organ Donor Card Request Hotline, 86
Orienteering, 63
The Orpheus Club, 25, 38
The Orton Dyslexia Society, 103
Other Addictions, 85
Outdoor Club of South Jersey, 55
Outdoor Singles, 49
Overeaters Anonymous, 85

P

PA Department on Aging, 102
PA Lawyer Referral Service, 104
Pals for Life, 77
Parent Action Network of Philadelphia, 98
The Parent Center, 99
Parent Education Network, 99
Parent Exchange, 90, 99, 103
Parent Resource Association Center, 99
Parent's Express Magazine, 125
Parent's Guide of Delaware Valley, 125
The Parents Guide to the Del. Val., 129
Parents in Progress, 99
Parents Inc., 99
Parents Network, 99, 103
Parents Project, 99
Parents Supporting Parents, 99, 103
Parents Without Partners, 49, 92, 100
Parents, Families & Friends of Lesbians & Gay, 108
Parkinson Disease, 88
PC User Group of South Jersey, 14
PCP Users Group, 14
Penguin Place, 109
Penn A & C Rowing Association, 65
Penn. Innovation Network, 10
Pennsylvania Angler Magazine, 125
Pennsylvania Assoc. for Blind Athletes., 75
Pennsylvania Ballet Company
   Corps De Voluntaires, 25
   Volunteer Guild, 25
The Pennsylvania Bar Association, 125
Pennsylvania Bike Club, 57
Pennsylvania Dept. on Aging, 115, 119
Pennsylvania Folklife Magazine, 126

Pennsylvania Game & Fish Magazine, 126
Pennsylvania Game News, 126
Pennsylvania Golfer Magazine, 126
Pennsylvania Horticultural Society, 42
Pennsylvania Magazine, 126
Pennsylvania Pro Musica, 24, 39
Pennsylvania Sportsman Magazine, 126
Pennsylvania Triathlon Club, 74
Pennsylvania Wineries, 143
People Network, 10
Phila. Area Handicapped Ski Club, 75
Phila. Board of Ed. Volunteer Services, 78
Phila. Convention & Visitors Bureau, 112
Phila. Lesbian & Gay Task Force, 109
Phila. Soc. for the Preservation of Landmarks, 14
Phila. Volunteer Lawyers for the Arts, 104
Philadelphia Opera Junior Guild, 25
Philadelphia Advertising Club, 10
Philadelphia Area Computer Society, 14
Philadelphia Area Disc Alliance, 59
Philadelphia Area Scrabble Club, 30
Philadelphia Art Alliance, 15
Philadelphia Assoc. of Part-Time Prof., 10
Philadelphia Astrological Society, 27
Philadelphia Bar Assoc. Legal Hotline, 104
Philadelphia Buddhist Association, 32
Philadelphia Business Journal, 126
Philadelphia Candlelighters, 90
Philadelphia Canoe Club, 58
Philadelphia Cares, 78
Philadelphia Ceili Group, 19
Philadelphia Chamber Music Institute, 40
Philadelphia Choral Alliance, 38
The Philadelphia Daily News, 126
Philadelphia Dance & Music Network, 15
Philadelphia Depth Chargers, 72
The Philadelphia Fencing Center, 58
Philadelphia Flower Show, 144
Philadelphia Folklore Project, 15
Philadelphia Folksong Society, 23
Philadelphia Gay Men's Chorus, 39
Philadelphia Gay News, 127
Philadelphia Girls Rowing Club, 65
Philadelphia Golfer Magazine, 127
Philadelphia Guild of Handweavers, 26
Philadelphia Help Group (herpes), 89
The Philadelphia Inquirer, 127
Philadelphia Kite Festival, 144
Philadelphia Magazine, 127
Philadelphia Make it a Night, 143

INDEX

The Philadelphia Opera Guild, 25
Philadelphia Restaurant School, 143
The Philadelphia Revels, 36, 38
   Christmas Revels, 147
   May Day Celebration with the Revels, 144
Philadelphia Rock Gym, 64
Philadelphia Sailing Club, 67
Philadelphia Science Fiction Society, 29
Philadelphia Ski Club, 69
Philadelphia Sports & Social Club, 55
Philadelphia Swing Dance Society, 21
Philadelphia Trail Club, 62
Philadelphia Visitors Center, 112
Philadelphia Weekly Newspaper, 127
Philadelphia with Children (a book), 129
Philadelphia Women's Network, 12
Philadelphia Writers Organization, 10, 21
Philadelphia Zoo, 41
Philanthropic Groups, 33, 42
Philomusica Chorale, 39
Phoenix Players, 36
The Photographic Society of Phila., 29
Photography, 29
Pick Your Own Fruit, 145
Pine Baron's Barbershop Chorus, 39
Pineland Country Dancers, 17
Places to go with Children in the Del. Valley, 129
Planetree Health Resource Ctr. Hotline, 86
Planned Parenthood, 107
Playcrafters, 36
Players Club, 36
Playmasters, 36
Plays & Players, 36
PLGTF Hotline, 107
Poconos Road Conditions Info., 140
Poetry, 21
Poetry and Literary Forum, 21
Point to Point at Winterthur, 144
Police Athletic League, 32
Port Indian Regatta/Hydroplane Races, 146
Port Indian Ski Club, 74
Positive Parenting, 100
Practical Parenting, 100
Pregancy Advice Hotline, 107
Professional & Business Singles Network, 49
Professional Singles Network Mag., 127
Professionals in Transition, 115

Prospective Small Business Owners, 105
Prospectors' Club of Cherry Hill, 10
Public Interest Law Ctr. of Phila., 104

Q

Quilters of the Round Table, 26
Quilting Guilds, 26

R

R.E.I. Sports Equipment, 64
The Radnor Hunt Fall 3-Day Event, 146
The Radnor Hotel, 143
Radnor Hunt Steeplechase Races, 145
Ralph Stover Climber Coalition, 64
Rape and Crime Victim Assistance, 109
Rape Crisis Center (South Jersey), 107
Rape Crisis Center Hotline, Montgomery County, 107
Rape Crisis Council Hotline, Chester County, 107
Rape Crisis Hotline, Delaware, 107
Rebuilding (a book), 131
Recovery, Inc., 88
Rehoboth Bay, 139
Religion, 32
Relocation Quarterly Magazine, 127
Republican Party, 43
Resolve, Inc., 100, 109
The Retired Senior Volunteer Program, 78
Ritz Theater, 36
Rock Climbing, 64
Roller Blading/Inline Skating, 64
Rose Valley Chorus & Orchestra, 37
Rose Valley Orchestra, 40
Rose Valley Pops, 40
Rosemont College Community Chorus, 24
Rotary Club, 34
Rowing Program for the Disabled, 75
Rowing/Sculling, 65
Running/Racewalking/Walking, 66

S

Saddle Club, 63
Sailing/Boating, 67
Salem Community Theater, 36
Samaritan Counseling Center, 85, 89, 91, 100, 108, 115, 118
Samuel S. Fleisher Art Memorial, 15
The Savoy Company, 37
Schuylkill River Greenway Association, 41
Science Fiction, 29

INDEX

Scrabble, 30
Scuba Diving, 72
Select Singles, 50
Senior Centers, 119
Senior Citizen Hotlines, 117
Senior Volunteers Needed, 78
Service Corps of Retired Executives, 78
Settlement Music School Opera Trips, 25
Sex and Love Addicts Anonymous, 86
Sexually Transmitted Diseases support, 89
Shalom Progam, 111
Shawnee Mountain, 142
Shore Cycling Club, 57
Sierra Club Singles, 50
Sierra Club, N.J., 62
Sierra Club, S.E. Pennsylvania, 62
Singing (Participatory), 24
Singing City, 24, 38
Single Booklovers, 50
The Single Gourmet, 50
Single Parent Activities and Programs, 100
Single Parents, 92
Single Parents Society, 50, 92, 100
Single Soilmates, 50
Single Vegetarians, 51
Singles, 51, 128
   Events and Seasonal Locations, 46
Singles at the Shore Magazine, 128
Singles Interdenominational, 51
Singles Magazine, 128
Singles Ministries (in general), 49
Singles on Sailboats, 53
Singles Over 30, 51
The Singles Scene, 51
Skate Dawgz, 64
Sketch Club Players, 36
Ski Club of Delaware Valley, 71
Skiing:
   Snow, 68
   Water, 74
Small Business Administration, 106
Small Business Assoc. of Del. Valley, 10
Small Business Owners Support, 105
Smocking Arts Guild of America, 26
Smoke Stoppers, 84
Smokenders, 84
Smokers Anonymous, 84
Smoking Addiction, 84
The Snoball, 71, 146
Snowdrifts Magazine, 128
Society of American Magicians, 29

Society of Young Magicians, 29
Song Writer's Forum, 23
Song Writing (Participatory), 23
Sons of the Desert, 28
Soroptimist Int'l of the Americas, 34
South Jersey Apple/Mac User Group, 14
South Jersey Business Journal, 126
South Jersey Entrepreneurs Network, 10
South Jersey Pops Orchestra, 40
South Jersey Scrabble Club, 30
South Jersey Single Professionals, 51
South Jersey Ski Club, 71
South Jersey Wheelmen, 57
Special Interest Personals (descrip.), 134
The Special Olympics, 42
Sports
   All Varieties of Sports, 54
   Bicycling, 56
   Boardsailing, 74
   Boating, 67
   Canoeing, 58
   Disc Golf, 59
   Fencing, 58
   Frisbee Golf, 59
   Frisbee, Frisbee Golf, Disc Golf, 59
   Golf, 59
   Hiking, 61
   Horseback Riding, 63
   In-line Skating, 64
   Orienteering, 63
   Racewalking, 66
   Rock Climbing, 64
   Roller Blading/Inline Skating, 64
   Rowing/Sculling, 65
   Running, 66
   Sailing, 67
   Scuba Diving, 72
   Snow Skiing, 68
   Sports for the Physically Handicapped, 75
   Surfing, 72
   Swimming, 72
   Table Tennis, 73
   Tennis, 73
   Triathlon, 74
   Walking, 66
   Water Skiing, 74
   Windsurfing, 74
Sports After Dark, 143
Spotlighters, 36
Spring Mountain, 142
St. Andrews Players, 36

INDEX

St. Dorothy's Singles Group, 50
St. Peter's Young Adults, 50
St. Thomas Players, 36
Stage Magazine, 35, 128
Stagecrafters, 36
Stamp Collecting, 30

Standard Rate and Data Services, 130
The Starting Point, Inc., 86
State Health Hotline, 86
Sterling Community Chorus, 39
Strive (for young stroke victims), 88
Stuttering, 103
Suburban Cyclists Unlimited, 58
Suburban Philadelphia Video Club, 29
Sudden Infant Death Syndrome Foundation, 92
Suicide & Crisis Intervention Hotline, 83, 94, 107
Summer Beach Events, 146
Summer Hang-outs:
   The Delaware Shore, 139
   The Jersey Shore, 138
   Other Options, 140
   The Poconos, 139
Sunrise Network, 11
Sunset Beach, 139
Supportive Older Women's Network, 109
Surf Anglers Association, 28
Surfing, 72
Survivors of Suicide, 93
Swedish Historical Museum, 76
Sweet Adelines Chorus, 39
Swimming, 72
Symphony Club, 40

T

Table Tennis, 73
The Tail Waggers Club, 51
Take a Hike Club, 62
Talk Cinema (Harlan Jacobson's), 22
Talking Yellow Pages Hotlines, 110
Teamworks, 11
Temple Elderly Law Project, 104
Temple Sinai Singles Forum, 51
Temple Support Groups, 90
Temple Univer., Sm. Bus. Devel. Ctr., 105
Tennis, 73
Tennis Parties in Princeton, 73
Tenth Presbyterian Church Singles, 52
Theatre Center Playwrights, 21

Theatre:
   Non-Participatory, 24
   Participatory, 35
THEOS, 93
Thespis Inc., 36
Things to do on New Year's Eve, 148
The Thrift Shop Maniac's Guide, 129
Tips:
   How to Use This Book, 6
   How to Write/Answer a Personal Ad, 131
To Live Again, 93
Toastmasters International, 11
Toughlove International, 100
Tower Club of Philadelphia, 52
Town & Country Players, 36
Tradeswomen of Phila./Women in Non-trad. work, 115
Transitional Dining Club, 52
Travel, 76
Travel Information Center (for handicapped), 103
Travelers Aid Society, 110
Tri-State Singles, 52
Triathlon Club, 74
Trout Unlimited & Fly Fishers, 28
Tuesday Night Square Dance Guild, 20
25 Bicycle Tours of Eastern PA, 130

U

Undine Barge Club, 65
Unite, Inc., 93
Univ. of PA Sm. Business Devel. Ctr., 105
University Barge Club, 65
University of Penn. Outdoor Club, 63

V

Valborgsmassoafton Festival, 144
Valley Forge Computer Club, 14
Valley Forge Golf Club, 60
Valley Forge Signal Seekers, 27
Variety Club, 42
Vegetarian Singles, 52
Vegetarian Society of South Jersey, 30
Vegetarians of Philadelphia, 31
Vesper Boat Club, 65
Video, 29
Video Dating Services (description of), 135
Village Playbox, 36
Village Players of Hatboro, 36
Villanova Athletic Club, 67
Villanova Theater, 36

INDEX

Villanova Univ., Sm. Business Institute, 105
Vintage Magazine, 128
Visions Magazine, 128
Visitors Ctr. (for Independence Park), 112
Volleyball for Singles, 52
The Volunteer Action Council, 78
Volunteer Fire Departments, 78

W

Walking Club for Older Adults, 63
Wanderlust Hiking Club, 63
Warminster, 40
Warminster Community Theater, 36
Warmline (childcare questions), 94
Washington Crossing the Del., 148
Waterfront Table Tennis Club, 73
Wayne Oterie, 40
Weekenders, 52
Welcome Wagon Club of Media, 112
Welcome Wagon Club of North Penn, 112
Welcome Wagon International, 111
Well Spouse Foundation, 101
West Chester Barley Sheaf Players, 36
West Chester U., Sm. Business Devel. Ctr., 106
West Jersey Ski Club, 70
Where the Personal Ads are Found, 134
White Clay Bicycle Club, 58
Widow & Widower, 93
Widows or Widowers Club, 52
Wilmington Drama League, 36
Wilmington Ski Club, 71
Wilmington Trail Club, 63
Windsurfing, 74
Wishcraft (a book), 131
Wissahickon Off-Road Cyclists, 58
Wissahickon Ski Club, 70
Women Against Abuse, 109
Women Against Abuse Hotline, 107
Women Against Abuse Legal Center, 105
Women for Sobriety, 84
Women In Transition, 86, 93, 109
Women In Transition Hotline, 107
Women Organized Against Rape, 110
Women Organized Against Rape Hotline, 107
Women's Ctr. of Montgomery Cnty, 110, 115
Women's Law Project, 105
Women's Opportunity Center, 116
Women's Opportunity Resource Ctr., 116
Women's Referral Network of Chester County, 12
The Women's Resource Ctr., 93, 110, 116
The Women's Yellow Pages, 130
Woodland Avenue Players, 36
Workplace, 116
World Affairs Council of Philadelphia, 43
Wreck Raiders Scuba Club, 73
Writer's Club of Delaware County, 21

Y

Yardley Players, 36
YM & YWCA, 32, 54, 119
YM & YWHA, 32, 54, 119
Young Democrats, 43
Young Friends of:
  Brandywine River Museum, 22
  Philadelphia Museum of Art, 23
  Philadelphia Opera, 25
  Philadelphia Orchestra, 25
Young Jewish Adults of Delaware, 52
Young Jewish Leadership Council, 53
Young Members:
  Phila. Soc. for Preserv. of Landmarks, 14
  Variety Club, 42
Young Republicans, 43
Young Widow & Widower, 93
Youth & Family Services, NJ Southern Region, 85, 89, 91, 101, 108, 115, 118
Youth & Family Services, NJ State Hotline, 85, 89, 91, 101, 108, 115, 118
Youth Crisis Line, 83, 94
YWCA Resource Center, 116

Z

Zagat Survey (a book), 130
The Zipper Club, 88
Zoobilee, 145